Training and Transfer of Learning

FARHAD ANALOUI
Development and Project Planning Centre
University of Bradford

Avebury

Aldershot · Brookfield USA · Hong Kong · Singapore · Sydney

Published by
Avebury
Ashgate Publishing Limited
Gower House
Croft Road
Aldershot
Hants GU11 3HR
England

Ashgate Publishing Company
Old Post Road
Brookfield
Vermont 05036
USA

ˌ0000ו5560

A CIP catalogue record for this book is available from the British Library and the US Library of Congress.

ISBN 1 85628 009 3

Printed and Bound in Great Britain by
Athenaeum Press Ltd., Newcastle upon Tyne.

Contents

CHAPTER TWO: Training and learning

CHAPTER THREE: Training methods and transfer

CHAPTER FOUR: Socialisation: An invisible learning programme

CHAPTER FIVE: A socio-technical explanation for transfer of learning

CHAPTER SIX: Effective transfer and its scopes and limitations

CHAPTER SEVEN: The future of transfer

Bibliography

Preface

Whilst the concept of learning constitutes the most well known topic of enquiry for researchers, academics, students and even the layman, its transfer has remained relatively neglected and unexplored particularly in relation to the most inevitable organisational activity - training. Unfortunately, this subject has traditionally been treated in isolation from the reality of the work organisation.

The transfer of learning is a necessity without which the success of a training programme and indeed the effectiveness and efficiency of an organisation as a whole can not be guaranteed.

The recent resurgence of interest in the subject of transfer of learning, particularly in the context of training, has been partly brought about by the relatively low success rate and even down right failure of a vast number of training programmes.

This book examines the problem of transfer from a socio-technical perspective, one which regards the transfer of learning, especially in the context of the organisation, as a socio-psychological phenomenon which needs to be addressed as a process which is initiated by 'learning' and which extends to 'doing'.

I would like to thank Professor David Edwards and Dr. John Wiess for their constructive comments. I would also like to thank Mr Bill Page for allowing me to use excerpts from my articles which have appeared in the Journal of Project Appraisal and Mr John Ankers from ICI Huddersfield. I am particularly indebted to my wife for her relentless efforts and support during the preparation of the many drafts of the manuscript and Sue Mackrill for her pleasant, professional and creative approach to the production of the diagrams and the final camera ready copy of the manuscript.

1 Transfer: A problematic issue

Introduction

In most organisations, large and small, in private or public sector, in order to ensure that the employees continue to perform or behave at the predetermined and desired level, some form of training or retraining programme has to be periodically used.

It is now well recognised that training can not only be employed as a means of improving the performance of the unskilled, semi-skilled or skilled employees, but can also be used as a powerful tool to improve the knowledge and skills of managers and for developing their managerial potential and ability so that the organisation, as a whole, may benefit from their increased effectiveness.

It is assumed that improved performance on the part of the employees leads to a more efficient organisation. Since efficiency implies an increase in the ratio of the output in relation to input, efficient organisations are expected to produce more product or provide more and better services (output) at a lower cost. It is even suggested that training no longer needs to be seen as a long term investment, for with an efficient and effective training programme, the dividends can appear in a matter of months (Mills, 1972).

The concern which was shown by executives, management consultants,

1

share holders and politicians alike throughout the 80's for improved effectiveness on the part of employees and organisations as a whole, is likely to remain as strong during the 90's and beyond. The emphasis will be placed on leaner organisations with the optimum use of resources human or otherwise, in order to achieve higher rates of productivity and profitability. The preoccupation with efficiency will continue to form the basis for managing organisations and will undoubtedly form the working norms for their managers.

> Successful companies stress training both as a way of increasing efficiency and as a means of instilling the company's values into its employees. Although many such employees may not be exceptional, the successful companies get from them an extraordinary level of performance (Bennett, 1988, p.1).

Training provides the necessary bridge or, at least, the most popular means for filling the gap between the present actual level of performance of the employees and their desired level of performance, which would guarantee the realisation of the above objectives. That is, an increased level of effectiveness on the part of the people who work for the organisations, the subsequent rise in the efficiency of the work organisations and the benefits which this will yield.

Peters and Waterman, in their famous book 'In Search of Excellence', while pointing out the importance of the role of effective management and their contribution towards the organisations effectiveness, where they carried out their research, note that, 'There are enough signs of training intensity to state that training was highly related to organisational excellence...' (1982, p.142).

It is not surprising to see that a staggering amount of money is spent annually on training and development in order to ensure that, in a continual search for increased effectiveness and efficiency in the face of ever diminishing natural resources and opportunities, so that a competitive edge amongst rivals and competitors is maintained. Like it or not, the training and development of the human resources available to us, as a business strategy, will still remain an effective option, if not the most economical alternative, towards ensuring the present survival of the enterprise and its progress in the future. Sound and relevant training and development programmes can prepare the people in organisations to face the socio-economic uncertainty and successfully cope with the ever increasing technological change.

2

ICI, an international chemical group, with 132,000 employees, manufactures in 40 countries and sells in 150. It is a fine example of an international enterprise which values training and development, for its employees and managers, as a viable means towards securing a competative edge amongst its rivals worldwide.

> ICI's competative edge depends on the talents of its people. Through its structur, its policies and the training and opportunities it offers, ICI seeks to ensure that all employees are given every chance to develop their talents (ICI World Data, 1991, p.19).

Training and development constitutes a major item in the manifestos of the political parties, not just in Britain and other Western technologically advanced nations, but also amongst the developing nations throughout the world.

Bennett reports, '...UK is pouring massive amounts of money into vocational youth training. In Singapore it has been recognised that increased skills are needed to sustain or improve national performance and to move away from a low-image economy' (1988, p.1).

Naturally, the reader's immediate response to this would be that, if training can deliver what is needed in industry and can fulfil the promise of higher productivity, effectiveness and proficiency, so what seems to be the problem? What is not often recognised is that training can only constitute a viable solution to inefficiency and low productivity if and only if it can be transferred to the job. There are certain aspects, such as the transfer of learning, which is inherent in the process of training and development and which requires a great deal of attention and thinking through, if training as an intervention is to be effective. The fact is that frequently the effectiveness of the training itself has to be questioned.

Lynton and Pareek assert that, 'No one doubts the contribution that training can make to the development of all kinds. Training is essential, obviously so. Doubts arise only over the contribution in practice. Complaints are growing about its effectiveness and waste' (1990, p.3).

Training and transfer

The terms training and development have become popularly and commonly used by non specialists as meaning 'learning to do something' and more often than not, it is associated with learning to do a 'job' in a place of work. To avoid any misunderstanding and to ensure that the reader, the scholar and practitioner, understand the important relationship between the issue of transfer and training, it is deemed necessary to define the term training.

The recent explosion of literature on the subject means that training is defined by different writers to explain its relevance to a specific task, (eg fire fighting), for operators (eg tool makers), a specific subject matter (eg medicine), in relation to certain role occupiers (eg production manager), and specific field (eg management). There are also other classifications, such as induction, main and follow up training which have been used as a basis for its definition. Naturally, each definition offers different slants in describing what training is supposed to be.

To the non-specialist, it may come as a surprise to learn that, for example, in England training is defined differently than the definition which is used in the USA. The Department of Employment Glossary of Training Terms (1971) offers the definition, 'The systematic development of the attitude/knowledge/skill or behaviour pattern required by an individual to perform adequately a task or job'. The emphasis is placed on the systematic approach, individual and not necessarily group training. Finally, the most important aspect of this definition which will be negated in this book and which directly influences the degree of effective transfer, is the over emphasis which is placed on the success of training programmes as being solely measured by the improved task-related performance of the trainees involved.

In contrast with the above, the typical American definition places more emphasis on the organisation, support for training, people and the overall effectiveness of the enterprise. For example, training is referred to as 'Any organisationally initiated procedures which are intended to foster learning amongst organisational members in a direction contributing to organisational effectiveness' (Hinichs, 1976).

Other writers tend to place emphasis on the processes involved in the training activity, rather than who the training programme is designed for. Pepper (1984), defines training as 'that organised process [which is] concerned with the acquisition of capability, or the maintenance of an existing capability' (p.9).

I believe that for a better understanding of the issue of transfer and its significance and relevance for the effectiveness of a training programme, the adoption of a view which offers wider applications and which is trainee (individual or group) orientated is required. Such a view should also direct the attention towards the ultimate purpose of any training activity - the contribution which is directly or indirectly made to the effectiveness of the organisation. However, that should not mean that attention should solely be paid to the task-related aspect of a training programme at the expense of excluding vital processes such as learning and the transfer of that learning to the actual workplace. Therefore, in agreement with Bramley (1991, p.XV), a viable definition of the subject should include the following;

1. Systematic processes which are concerned with some form of planned and controlled, rather than random learning experience.

2. Changing the behaviour, skills and attitudes of people as individuals and as members of social work groups.

3. Improvement of both the present and the following job performance (effective transfer) and enhancement of the effectiveness of the organisation in which the individual or group works.

As it will be made clear, the overall effectiveness of the trainees may not necessarily be related solely to the improved task performance but could also be due to their social competence and skills. A crucial point which is not adequately dealt with where discussions concerning the definition of training have been cited in the literature.

Why ineffective training?

So how can training become ineffective and thus lead to the wastage of resources which otherwise could have been spent on, for example, recruitment of new employees with the desired level of skills and competence which the organisation requires? Or alternatively such wasted funds could have been spent on reward schemes of a kind which would improve productivity. The answer to the above question, which has become a major preoccupation for Human Resource Development (HRD) specialists and personnel practitioners, is that there are many factors which could be identified as having negative influence on the training programme and thus cause the programme not to achieve its set objectives. To name a few; incorrect identification and analysis of the training needs; inapt choice of training method; inappropriate design of the training programme and learning activities; irrelevant content and weak structure of the programme; unsuitable structure of the learning situation; failure to identify and assess the capacity of the individual learners, the nature of their past learning experiences and their capability for learning and relearning the material and the acquisition of the skills to which they are exposed; and finally, unqualified trainers and the lack of a sound evaluation procedure. These factors can individually or collectively

5

contribute to ineffective training programmes.

Indeed, in the words of an experienced trainer, 'there are a thousand and one things which could go wrong during any training and learning situation which could potentially, either individually or cumulatively result in the failure of a training programme'. The intention here is not to list all such contributing factors. These have mostly been dealt with elsewhere. The aim is to focus on the issue which is often neglected when a training programme is terminated, after the evaluation is carried out and the individual trainees have been physically transferred to the job situation. The author is interested in whether or not the learning which has taken place during the training can effectively be materialised on the job.

The concern here is with the issue of 'transfer', because the observations made in industry, the numerous accounts provided by practicing trainers, personnel specialists and managers and the reports cited in the literature, all indicate the neglect which transfer has suffered and the fact that even now very little is known about this elusive phenomenon - the transition of the learnt material to the workplace environment. Haslerud (1972) asserts, 'Many in psychology and education have admitted that transfer is at once the most important and the most neglected part of the psychology of learning' (p.viii).

Never the less, it is important to note that, in my view, the concern for transfer should not be limited to remembering and retaining certain abstract material or knowledge and skills per se. When it comes to training situations, transfer encompasses a wide spectrum of activities, skills, knowledge and complex processes which should also include consideration of the values, behaviours and expectations of the trainers and the prospective employers both during the training and after it is terminated. The behavioural or attitude changes induced, or indeed the lack of them, as a result of exposure to a training activity, in terms of the performance, attitudes and orientation of the people at work, needs to be included in the analysis of the transfer.

To this extent I believe, whether - as shown in Figure 1.1 - training takes place outside of the physical environment of the workplace and is then expected to be transferred to the workplace or that the training is conducted within the workplace, either on the job or near it, transfer ought to be seen as one of the single most important determining factors in the effectiveness of training programmes.

It is, however, crucial to remember that transfer ought to be viewed in the 'context of training', one which commences from the training situation and one which will mature and hopefully be realised within the workplace

6

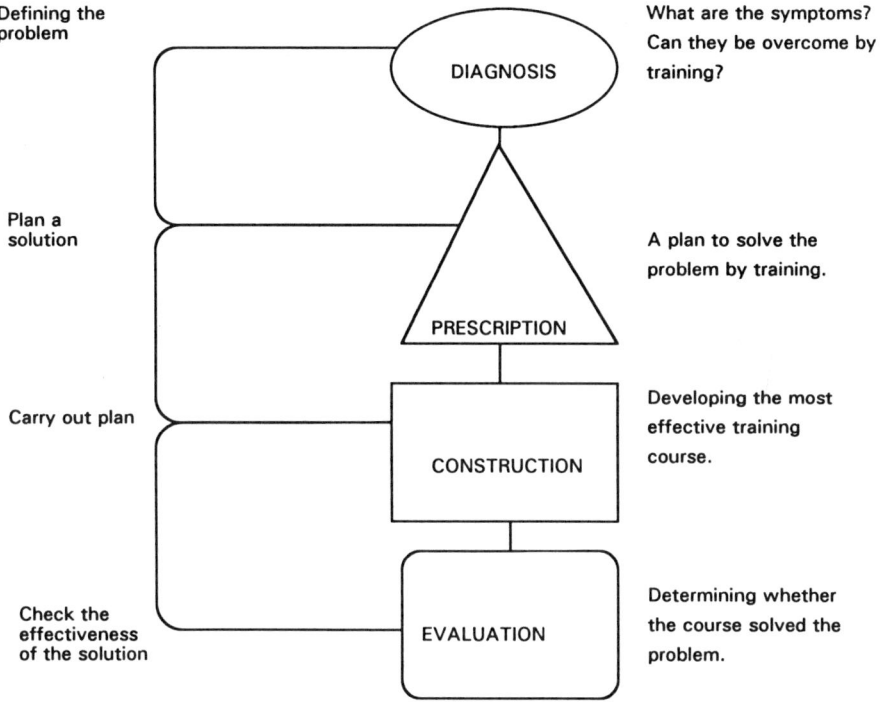

Defining the problem	DIAGNOSIS	What are the symptoms? Can they be overcome by training?
Plan a solution	PRESCRIPTION	A plan to solve the problem by training.
Carry out plan	CONSTRUCTION	Developing the most effective training course.
Check the effectiveness of the solution	EVALUATION	Determining whether the course solved the problem.

Figure 1.1   Sheffield System

Source: The above diagram is borrowed from E. Henry Hudson in
"Organisation of Training" by Davis (1973, p.37).

environment. The reality is that transfer occurs outside and beyond the traditionally perceived parameters of a typical training model characterised by the following four major stages as suggested by Davis (1973).

Diagnostic stage   Where the problem related to the behaviour, performance and productivity of the individual employee is assessed and defined in relation to what is expected from him (the desired state).   The usual question asked is, what are the symptoms and how can they be overcome by training?

Prescriptive stage Once the decision is made that the identified problems or deficiencies can be resolved or dealt with by some kind of training activities, a programme is then put together with the aim that the end result will ultimately create change in the behaviour or performance of the respective employee.

At this stage many issues will be of concern for the ultimate beneficiaries, the employer and the organisation as a whole. For example, what is the cost involved? Would such an expense be value added and justifiable, or should other alternatives be considered? At this stage of analysis the employees (trainees) are only considered in terms of numbers and maybe names. They are not yet exposed to the learning experiences and activities as prescribed in the form of a plan.

Construction stage This stage is concerned with developing the most effective training method and learning situation in which the optimum acquisition of the required knowledge and skills, attitude and behaviour can be guaranteed.

Of course, there are a variety of methods and techniques which could be employed for the purpose of conducting a training programme. The decision as to what method is to be used for implementing a training programme and the proximity of the venue to the actual workplace, as will be demonstrated, will have a significant effect on the degree of transfer which can be expected to occur at the end of the training programme.

What is, however, widely recognised by trainers and educators, is that some methods of training produce a smaller degree of transfer problems than others. It has been claimed that this could be due to the differences in the nature of the task-related (the technical aspects of the job) content of the training programme.

It is at this stage of planning and designing a training programme that traditionally trainers and educators conveniently assume that by carrying out training need analysis methodologically and by ensuring that the content matter is relevant to the needs of the individuals, transfer will automatically occur once the training is over. Regretfully, it has been observed on numerous occasions that the choice of the method used in implementing a training programme, in particular, and the other factors listed above have not been considered with the reality of actual workplace in mind.

Evaluation stage Typically the training programme is evaluated at the end. In almost all training programmes, whether operative training or management development, some form of evaluation is included. The

8

success and failure of the programme is usually determined by deciding on whether or not the intended learning has taken place. The irony is that although evaluation exercises can tell us, albeit with a certain limited degree of accuracy, what has been learnt -internalisation - such activities can reveal very little, if anything at all, about the extent to which the learnt material can be guaranteed to be transferred effectively to the actual job situation. Yet, for most trainers and training centres, evaluation often marks the end of the process.

Observation has shown that the end of course evaluation exercise has gradually changed meaning to become nothing but a ritual which is religiously adhered to by all trainers and educators. It is rumoured that evaluation activities are undertaken by trainers in order to justify the need for their own presence, rather than measuring the degree of usefulness of and applicability to the job of what has been learnt. The concern for the end results which ought to be the maximisation of the transfer of learnt material to the job situation is conveniently overlooked.

This purely technical (task-related) approach to training places stress solely on what an individual has to learn in order to do a job at the workplace. For example, a joiner learns to construct wooden frames, an accountant learns how to do double entry book keeping or a manager who works for a small processing enterprise should learn about the chemical processes and other related technical activities which take place in his job; or a lecturer who teaches management development learns about the concepts, theories and techniques, of a traditional and contemporary nature, which are recommended as part of the necessary knowledge and attributes for teaching and educating prospective managers.

> At the conceptual level, the goal is to specify which training procedure can optimise the transfer [of task-related knowledge and skills] and from that develop functions which permit trade-off estimates to be made for a particular situation (Cormier and Hagman, 1987, p.3).

In practice, the success or failure of the training is assessed by the degree of the success or failure which is displayed by the trained individuals in their jobs. The traditional approach to explaining transfer tends to regard the trainees' overall effectiveness in terms of the ability and skills on their part to carry out solely the technical aspects of the job, as though the individuals concerned live and work in a social vacuum.

Not only has this purely task-related approach to transfer failed to provide a satisfactory explanation for what is observed after a training programme is terminated, but it also tends to trivialise the significance of the socialisation processes which occur both during and after the training programme. Fleishman (1953), talks of a management training course which was arranged for the foremen of an engineering company who showed satisfactory progress immediately after the completion of the leadership training, but not at the follow up stage some time after the re-entry to the shop floor. He concludes that the attitude of the immediate manager towards the foreman, whether he was a considerate manager or otherwise, had a profound effect on the attitude that the foremen adopted in dealing with the work force. Davies (1971) also concludes that, 'The formal training [the task-related aspects] was only effective in those departments of the organisation which favoured the objectives of the course, in the other departments training had a contrary effect' (p.66).

Based on extensive observations made in industry, the author is now convinced that a more realistic approach towards achieving effective training needs to be adopted. Such an approach, as will be discussed in detail in the rest of this volume, requires attention being paid to both the social and technical aspects of training in order to pin-point the facilitative or inhibitive factors which are present in the learning situations and the organisation and which determine the degree of the transferability and applications of the learning to actual work situation (Analoui, 1990, p.175).

Beyond the training programme

On completion of a typical training programme, evaluation exercises are undertaken to assess the degree of success of a training programme in terms of improving the performance of the trainees involved. Should the trainee's performance be viewed as 'satisfactory', he or she is accordingly certified and sent to their respective workplace environment in the hope that the individual will perform as expected.

However, in the same way that the organ received by a transplant patient may only continue to function satisfactorily for a short time after the operation, often the trainees too, when transferred from the training situation into the actual workplace, may not perform at the level which was achieved whilst in the learning situation. This problem has come to be known as the 'problem of transfer'.

The programme has run its course. The participants are leaving on their way back to their job. They will now 'show what they have learnt. If the programme was full-time and residential going back to work is a major event. If it was long and located away, perhaps abroad, everything conspires to magnify the change over' (Lynton and Pareek, 1978, p.299).

Conventionally, substantial emphasis has been placed solely on the cognitive and behavioural aspects of the learning which takes place on training programmes. These include processes involved in the acquisition of new skills, knowledge, attitudes and behaviours.

As McGhee and Thayer (1961), aptly comment, 'Too often we stop paying attention to the trainee once the job is learnt, whether this learning has taken place within the classroom or on-the-job. The transition from 'learning' to 'doing' may well be the most crucial and most neglected phase of the training problems' (p.173).

In agreement with Trost, the author believes that having accepted that training is a planned and purposeful activity and that it is of value to the organisation, 'our concern should be with transferability of the learnt skills to the job' (1985, p.78). Moreover, it is worth noting that the traditional belief held by some trainers, that the transition of learnt knowledge and skills follows automatically, is nonsense and no rational basis can be found for it. Special effort ought to be made by trainees, trainers and those in charge in the organisation (the final destination) to facilitate and accelerate the process of transfer which relates the learning processes with training activities and links what goes on in the training situations with what actually occurs in the workplace environment, where the task has to be accomplished.

Thus, careful attention needs to be paid to 'the task of transferring and applying the new learning to within the trainee's work environment' (Analoui 1989, p.36). Otherwise as Robinson (1985) report, 'Too often employees attend a training programme, find the skills valuable, but don't use them on the job. There has been no transfer of the skills and knowledge acquired. Everyone, the organisation, the trainer and the employee, loses' (p.82).

The neglected aspects of transfer

There is no doubt that trainers and educators are concerned with what

11

happens after the final course of a training programme is over. Too many instances have been observed and numerous reports have been documented whereby trainees after completing a successful course of skills or knowledge acquisition have failed to incorporate what they have learnt into their actual work.

Many would argue that the 'transfer of training is not a neglected issue', by virtue of the fact that it is often talked about as a problem and has been the concern of serious trainers for many years. Yet, as it will be shown;
a) the debate concerning transfer is saturated with uncertainty, ambiguity and confusion;
b) only the learning situation is blamed for the lack of transfer; and
c) more often than not, the organisation - the actual workplace - is not seen as a main culprit or determining factor in relation to effective transfer and effective training, as the whole. Moreover, transfer as an issue is often seen and dealt with in an isolated manner, associated only with the learning which is often assumed to take place mainly in the training situation and not necessarily occurring within the actual work environment, well after entry or re-entry into the organisation.

Often post-training evaluations are carried out immediately after the trainees arrival back in the work situation when, as some practitioners put it, 'the dust has not settled yet'. In the analysis, transfer is not treated as a complex process which encompasses individual abilities, learning processes and situations, previous and present experiences, individual expectations and their unique frames of references, the organisation and motivational factors within the work environment.

This is particularly evident from the way in which transfer has been defined; 'the final phase in the training cycle is the incorporation into normal work of the new ways of thinking or carrying out tasks' (Bramely, 1991, p.26). Transfer has been dealt with as a detached stage in the training programme and not as what it is - a process.

In the training literature it is frequently observed that it is the nature of the skills and knowledge or the kind of values which are expected to be transferred to the workplace which have been the focus of attention, rather than the process of the transfer itself. This highlights the difficulty which has been experienced by the theorists and writers on the subject, to clearly relate the theory and practice together when defining transfer. For example, English and English (1958) note, 'Transfer is a general term for change in ability to perform a given act as a direct consequence of having performed another act relevant to it'. Such a definition doesn't indicate, for example, whether the transfer expected is the direct consequence of the 'perception of the task or only to its operation as a response that the transfer functions' (Haslerud, 1972, p.5). Nor does it consider the organisational context in which the transfer of the learnt skills, knowledge or attitudes and values is expected to occur.

At a practical level too, transfer is defined in isolation from the realities of the workplace. For example, in the Glossary of Training Terms, 1971, transfer is defined as 'that which occurs whenever the existence of a previously established habit or skill has an influence upon the acquisition, performance or re-learning of another habit or skill', (Stammer and Patrick, 1975, p.96).

Sometimes the activities and learning which had taken place previously have been included in the analysis. For example, Cormier and Hagman (1987) assert, 'In essence, transfer of learning occurs whenever prior learned knowledge and skills affect the way in which new knowledges and skills are learnt and performed' (p.1). Such attempts, as commented on earlier, tend to ignore the post training activities and learnings which occur in the workplace. Such organisationally related learnings may seem, at first, totally unrelated to the subject and content of the training programme, but they do effect the degree of the effective transfer on the job.

Before including some major classifications of this elusive phenomenon, it is worth reiterating that more often than not, an implicit assumption on the part of trainers and organisers regarding the learning experience is that, 'on changing from the simulated [training situation] to the real situation [actual workplace] the trainee will perform at an acceptable level' (Stammer and Patrick, 1975, p.96).

As Bramely aptly discerns, 'Often this is left to the individual, the implication being that the individual has the motivation and the ability to introduce such changes' (1991, p.25). In my view, a working definition for the practitioner ought to emphasise on transfer as being a process which begins with the individual or group and concerns the ability and motivation to learn in a particular learning situation and which concerns the extent to which the learnt knowledge and acquired skills can be seen to materialise, [this includes suitable changes in behaviour and attitudes as well as more evident changes in performance], within the working environment and consequently contributes to the effectiveness of the individual concerned, the unit, department or organisation as a whole.

To date, most available classifications have been developed by psychologists and educationalists whose main concern has been with the complex processes of learning, retention and memory. Stress, therefore, has been placed on motor, cognitive and metacognitive processes and their measurement in relation to the methodologies used for validating the experiments which were carried out. Not all such means are either relevant to the discussion of transfer of training or are they necessarily found useful by the practitioners in the field.

The serious reader will find terms such as 'negative' and 'positive' transfer liberally used in the relevant literature and training text books. The explanation offered for these terms is rather simplistic. When learnt knowledges and acquired skills are observed to be performed as expected, the transfer is regarded as positive and in cases where the trainee has not satisfactorily displayed the newly acquired skills, behaviour and competence the transfer is described as negative.

Transfer can be classed as 'specific' when it concerns knowledge, skills and values which are of a similar or exact nature to those found in the workplace or, on the other hand, it can be described as 'general' in that the material, skills and values learnt affect a wide range of new performance situations (Holding, 1965).

Psychologists are amongst those who believe in the principles of positive or negative transfer for predicting the degree of transfer. They generally place emphasis on analysis of the similarities which exist between the original performance and the improved task performance, the condition and level of training and the ability of the trainee.

The validity of psychological tests is often questioned. For example, Miner (1969) maintains that although these tests are valid in relation to the initial training period, they often do not accurately predict the extent to which the acquired 'learnt' material can be transferred to the job situation. Such findings are often curiously qualified with comments such as, 'the transfer from training to the actual work situation may not be perfect' in many instances and that what is learnt during training may have very little relevance for job performance (Shiver, 1980).

By and large, psychologists and educationalists seem to be preoccupied with the theoretical rather than the practical aspects of transfer. Gagne (1970), for example, distinguishes between 'vertical' and 'lateral' transfer. Vertical transfer occurring when 'a skill or knowledge directly attributes to the subsequent acquisition or performance of a superordinate task or skill. Lateral transfer is a kind of generalisation that spreads over a broad set of situations at roughly the same level of complexity' (p.231). Thus, the development of the theory of transfer in the context of training has mainly derived from the gradual accumulation of systematic analysis of the individuals cognitive ability in terms of learning processes, the acquisition of knowledge, skills, attitudes and behaviours. As a result a great deal of material, mainly of a task-related nature, has been accommodated on the application of learning theories to organisational training.

Occasionally, however, the analysis is extended beyond the immediate learning situation. For example, Berne (1961) points out the importance of the cultural differences and differences in the attitude of the trainees towards learning and the nature of the task to be performed. Bramely (1991), goes as far as suggesting that self-efficiency is the key to increasing the likelihood of the new knowledge, skill or behaviour being learnt.

On the whole, research on the problem of transfer of training, however, has not yielded any clear cut results, indeed many of the findings have been contradictory (Davies, 1971, p.104).

Identical elements, concept learning and reinforcement

Traditionally three major principles have been regarded as having the most impact on the occurrence of positive transfer. The principles of transfer typically have been based on the notion of Stimulus-Response; the language of inference theory. They were originally derived from taxonomies developed by eminent psychologists and human learning researchers such as Pavlov (1927), Thorndike (1898), Osgood et al (1957), Skinner (1954) and Gagne (1970). These are:

The presence of identical elements

This is based on the assumption that if the response and stimuli have many elements identical to those in the transferred task, the individual who performs effectively in learning or training situations should do well in any other similar situation. That is to say, by maximising the similarity between the training situation and the job, the likelihood that effective transfer will occur becomes greater (Miner, 1969). This is very similar to the notion of specific or vertical learning. Also, when a task requires the

15

learner to make the same response to a new but similar type of stimuli, positive transfer is increased with the increasing similarity. For example, once an individual learns to stop at one red light it is very easy to learn to stop at all red lights despite differences in shade, location and surrounding environment.

On the other hand, when a task requires the learner to make a new or different response to the same stimulus, because of a lack of similarity of the response, transfer tends to be negative and increases as the response required becomes less similar (Stammer and Patrick, 1975; McGhee, 1958). Thus, it is believed that;

a) Under conditions of high response similarity, positive transfer is produced.

b) Also it is usually more difficult under this condition to obtain negative transfer in vertical learning than it is in motor skills learning (Ellis, 1965, p.75).

This is particularly relevant to situations where a simulator is used as a training device. The recommendation is that the stimuli and response components have to be analysed and then represented in the light of their potential 'transfer' effects.

The emphasis on concept learning

Writers such as Harlow (1949) and McGhee (1958) argue that once the underlying principle is learnt, for example, that anti-clockwise movement tends to unscrew, whereas clockwise movement tends to tighten, this principle can be applied to a variety of situations and objects.

'Concept learning' thus induces 'generalisation' and leads to the occurrence of 'lateral' transfer because the trainee understands the underlying concepts, principles or procedures which have wide implications. However, concept learning is not a 'cut and dried' fact and it certainly is not supported by sufficient empirical research as to which stage of transfer can be enhanced if concepts or principles are emphasised in training situations.

The need for reinforcement

Reinforcement is based on the motivational theories which suggest that a combination of practice and reward on producing a desired response, will ultimately lead to effective and prolonged transfer. One problem with this method is that both in the learning situation and the workplace

16

environment, instructors and managers tend to discontinue reinforcement, rewards in extrinsic forms   such as verbal support or monetary offerings as the learner or trainee becomes more skilled. It is usually assumed that the trainee knows what he is supposed to do and therefore no further attention is needed.

Hertzberg (1968) refers to this form of motivation as similar to offering 'jelly beans' to people in order to reinforce the desired response on their part. The drawback is that each subsequent response requires even more reinforcement. Thus, so long as 'jelly beans' are available and offered the responses will follow.

Other writers place emphasis on 'self-sufficiency', 'autonomy' and the 'meaningfulness' of the task for the learner. The argument being that individuals who are self motivated or find the task meaningful are more likely to transfer the knowledge and skills acquired to the job.

The 'knowledge of result' or systematic feedback which is provided to learners by trainers in the training situation or at work by managers, is also considered to result in the enhancement of positive transfer. It is believed that if the individual learner knows how well they are doing they will be more encouraged to continue to progress to the next stage of the job and thus will continue to manage their own progress. Effective communication on the part of the trainers, educators and managers could be said to act as a motivating factor for producing positive transfer.

The aims and organisation of the book

It is evident that most attempts which have been made to analyse and explain the effective transfer of learnt material from the training situation to the actual workplace have been in vain. The preoccupation, on the part of theorists and writers with what should be learnt, that is the limited range of skills required to do the job, has led to the kind of neglect that the subject has traditionally suffered. Indeed, little attention has been paid to the importance of the social organisation of learning and the reality of the workplace context in which transfer is expected to occur.

The aim, therefore, is to demonstrate, that while the task-related content of a training programme is obviously important, a viable solution for the problem of transfer of learning should include a better understanding of the factors, of both social and technical natures, which act as 'facilitators' or 'inhibitors' towards the realisation of effective transfer into the actual workplace.

Intensive and complicated daily interactions amongst the trainees and between them and other members of the organisation in the workplace constitute the basis for the formation of the organisation's social system. The social culture of the workplace which not only acts as a decisive and influential factor towards the learning of the job, but it also behaves as a powerful regulatory mechanism in so far as the ways in which 'things are done' in a particular work environment are concerned.

In agreement with Hayes (1990), 'Training can only be effective within an organisation framework which permits and promotes its efficiency. All the efforts of a training institute to change the individual will be in vain unless the trainee's employing organisation is able to absorb the changes which the returning trainee imports into the workplace' (p.42).

To achieve effective training, therefore, first as explained earlier in this chapter, the issue of transfer ought to be regarded as a process which begins with learning and will continue to be present even after learning is completed. Second , that such a process is of a socio-technical nature. This simply means that as well as learning the task, it is necessary that attention is paid to the social learning processes which the trainee needs to gain mastery of in order to ensure his or her survival in the work organisation. These will provide the basis for the discussions in the remaining chapters.

Chapter two The major learning theories, concepts and principles will be reviewed in Chapter Two. Here, the emphasis is placed on the learning theories, differences in the potential of the individual for learning and the approaches which are normally adopted in order to ensure that learning should take place.

The intention is to demonstrate that learning, whether in the form of a personal experience or as a part of a systematically designed procedure, constitutes the very first step towards ensuring that the of transfer to the workplace of materials, experiences, skills, behaviours and attitudes will successfully take place.

The individual abilities, potential and willingness to learn and our attitude and orientation towards him and the learning, as a whole, are thought to play a central role towards achieving effective learning.

Chapter three The location, where learning is expected to take place, is the main concern here. In Chapter Three, it is shown that training modes and their proximity to the actual workplace play a crucial role in terms of determining the degree of positive transfer to the job.

The methods and techniques available to trainers and educators will be divided into two main groups; on-the-job and off-the-job and they will be examined accordingly.

First, the relationship between the complexity of the task content and the proximity of the training location to the actual workplace is explored - whether the method used is an on-the-job or an off-the-job type. Then in a subsequent discussion, the potential of the different modes and techniques available for producing effective transfer is assessed.

Chapter four Traditionally, writers on transfer treated the learning processes as complete once the trainee enters the workplace. Largely the attempts to measure the amount of positive transfer have been based on the degree of improved performance (doing) which is displayed by the trainee involved. In contrast with the above, in Chapter Four it is argued that both in the training centre and in the workplace social learning processes will continuously take place. The extent and the implicit nature of the social processes which are believed to, directly or indirectly, act as inhibitive or facilitative factors for enhancing learning, as a whole, is examined in relation to the transferability of the learnt material to the actual workplace. Actual cases observed in industry and elsewhere in work organisations are used to demonstrate how the workplace can play a decisive role in whether or not people will effectively put to use the knowledge and skills which they have acquired.

Chapter five Based on the above, an explanatory model - socio-technical - to explain why transfer does or does not occur has been constructed. Here the identified principles are brought together and are then briefly examined. This is done in order to critically evaluate the significance of the role, if any, that individual methods and the location of training, inhibitive and facilitative processes present within the workplace will have in relation to the realisation of effective transfer.

Chapter six The scope and limitations of the socio-technical approach for explaining effective or ineffective transfer and its potential for teachers, trainers, educators and consultants, will be evaluated in Chapter Six. Here, four broad categories of factors will be considered - the learner, what is to be transferred, the trainer and the organisation. These are believed to constitute the major actors and components of the organisation of transfer.

While using examples of cases observed by practitioners within the field, practical guide-lines will be provided for those concerned with effective training.

With the growing importance of action learning as an alternative means for effective learning, the reasons for its effectiveness in the context of the socio-technical approach to training, will also be included in this chapter.

Chapter seven Finally, in Chapter Seven, the earlier discussions will be concluded and lessons learnt will be put into place to complete the jigsaw puzzle of transfer. Certain recommendations will be made for increasing the effectiveness of management and non-management training. It is stressed that in dealing with the issue of transfer, neither a purely theoretical approach to the subject nor the adoption of a solely practical stand would explain transfer in its entirety.

In short, the socio-technical approach to the analysis of transfer, set out in the above chapters, aims to explain the complex phenomenon of effective transfer as what it is. A dynamic process which includes the individual trainees, their learning and training situations, the trainers and other people in the organisation. In short, it is concluded that process of transfer extends to the workplace where not all the contributining factors to effective or ineffective transfer can be completely harnessed and brought under control.

2 Training and learning

Introduction

The concept of learning is one of the most crucial, pertinent and inseparable aspects of any training programme or indeed of any organisational activity. As Luthan (1981) aptly remarks, 'There is little organisational behaviour that is not directly or indirectly affected by learning' (p. 23). There is, however, a subtle difference between learning as a part of a training activity and learning in its organisational context. The difference being that in a training programme, learning is a designed activity, whereas, as in an organisational context people are exposed to intricate processes of learning in indirect or subtle and even unconscious ways, regularly and on a daily basis.

However, the term learning is commonly used by the lay person to mean what has been 'learnt', whereas a psychologist tends to emphasis on 'how it works' regardless of the end product. Indeed, psychologists and educationalists have been the main contributors, and certainly the forefathers of the development of the subject and it is, therefore, not surprising that their concern has been with the process of 'how it works', rather than what it leads to (Gross, 1991). It is not unjust to suggest that, in the debate concerning learning and its development, traditionally the preoccupation on the part of the writers, researchers and theorists has been more to do with 'learning' as a concept, rather than its applications for the effectiveness of training and its relevance for the organisational effectiveness as a whole (Golembueski, 1976).

In this chapter, our main concern is with the application of learning, its theories and principles, and the degree to which the learnt material, values and attitudes can be successfully transferred, or realistically speaking, are allowed to materialise on the job in the actual workplace.

Definitions of learning and concern for transfer

There are diverse views as to what learning is, and how it can be facilitated and ultimately transferred. For those writers whose chief concern is with training, the applications of learning theories and concepts and principles, are the most significant. They tend to define the subject with emphasis placed on the acquisition of skills, knowledge and ultimately change in habits, attitudes, values and behaviours.

Beach (1980) defines concept of learning as 'That human process by which skills, knowledge, habits and attitudes are acquired and utilised in such a way that behaviour is modified'. Since the processes of learning itself are not observable, learning has even been referred to as being a 'hypothetical state which can only be inferred from observation of observable performance' (Stammer and Patrick, 1975, p.23).

It has been increasingly observed that learning is being defined in the context of change. Kenney and Reid (1986) use the definition of learning which was originally offered by Bass and Vaughan (1966), that suggests, learning is a relatively permanent change in behaviour that occurs as a result of practice or experience, but Kenney and Reid appropriately add that they wish to emphasise 'Today [such change is the result] of learning from experience' (p.115). Gleuck also proposes that learning is 'the act by which an individual acquires skills, knowledge and the abilities which result in relatively permanent change' (1974, p324).

The difficulty, however, is to establish with certainty whether or not the changes have taken place and if they have, to what extent the planned changes aimed for through a training programme, are likely to be exhibited and displayed when the trainee assumes the actual work responsibility in the organisation. Hardy and Haze (1979) have partly demonstrated their concern for transfer in their definition of learning. They suggest 'learning involves changes of behaviour and presumably because the change of behaviour is relatively permanent, there must also be a relatively permanent change somewhere inside us which allows us, once we have learnt something, to demonstrate this learning again later' (p.67).

It was suggested in Chapter One, where the importance of learning was briefly discussed, particularly in the context of training activities, that the debate on learning as an aspect of training should inevitably include the organisation, both as a place in which the result of the learning is expected to occur and, even more importantly, as a place where after formal training is completed the individuals or groups are exposed to more continuous learning processes which determine whether or not the changes in the trainee's behaviour, attitude, knowledge or skills should be displayed or utilised on the job.

The irony is that since the conventional approach to the transfer of learning is mainly concerned with the observable behavioural changes, as being indicative of whether or not learning has taken place, when for reasons not apparent to us the individual trainee fails to display what has been learnt, it is usually the training centres and trainers which are blamed for the inadequacies and deficiencies observed in the trainee's performance. Worse even, it is suspected that no learning has taken place and that the trainee had not been able to acquire or retain the skills and knowledge expected from him.

It is not, therefore, an exaggeration to claim that the importance of learning for the trainers, specialists and practitioners is all too evident. Yet, the difficulty that most trainers and, in particular, practitioners often find themselves faced with is that 'unfortunately there is no single coherent body of learning theory. [There is] an assortment of theories [which] co-exist' (Jones, 1979, p,22). In fact, as Kenney and Reid (1986) aptly suggest there is no single 'all embracing theory of learning which will cover all situations' (p.118) which can be recommended. Nor is it possible to suggest a single piece of work which contains all that has so far been said on the subject of learning. Although there seems to exist, amongst the theorists and writers, a general agreement concerning the presence of some forms of principles of learning, there is still a wide spread disagreement on the theories behind them (Luthan, 1981).

Each theorist or group of theorists tends naturally to advocate or support a particular taxonomy which is believed to provide an adequate explanation or grounds for the 'prediction' of and the 'control' of learning, the learner and the learning situations.

There are various theories of learning, each of which have contributed, to some degree, to our present understanding of the concept. The inclusion of all theories, classifications, views and opinions on the subject of learning is neither necessary nor realistically practical. What, however, is thought to be beneficial is to briefly look at the developmental stages that learning has gone through to date, and analyse the principles and factors related to learning, both in the context of the training situation where the aim is to enhance the acquisition of knowledge and skills, as well as, facilitating the process of transfer to the workplace.

It is my belief that it would be more helpful to not just present the contributions made on the subject of learning but also to delve deeper and to consider the general assumptions which underlie these theories and assess the implications for the trainer, trainee as a learner, and the transfer of what is learnt; That is the out come of training, in the form of new, modified or changed behaviour within the workplace.

Milestones in the development of 'learning theories'

When reviewing the available literature on learning theories and training the most striking pattern is that of the presence of 'change'. Throughout the, relatively speaking, short history of learning theories there is a visible trend of gradual change in the paradymic position of the researchers and theorists concerned. As suggested by Burrel and Morgan (1979), 'when dealing with the understanding of [a subject], it is the underlying assumptions of the writers and theorists who have concerned themselves with a social phenomenon, which to a large extent determines their approach, their understanding and their explanation of social reality'.

One such underlying assumption is our view concerning 'Man', in our case the 'learner' or the 'trainee' involved. How do we perceive our role as trainers, instructors, advisers, facilitators and the like (Margerison, 1988) when we approach the work organisations, the learning situations, the implementation of training programmes and our expectations of a training programme once it is completed.

The above assumptions concerning the individual, learning, training and our roles as trainers, however, has been subjected to constant change. Indeed, the development of our views concerning learning and what it should be, in its present state, is a reflection of the change in our attitude which no doubt will go on to be questioned and changed again and again in the future.

Each theory or taxonomy of learning is that each tends to reveal only certain aspects of this complex and multi-dimensional phenomenon. For example, Miller (1967) in his analogy places emphasis on the psychological demands made on the trainee by the task. In doing so he poses an intriguing question. If a robot was expected to behave like a human being what function would have to be built into it? He then goes on to offer a five-stage taxonomy of learning.

Concept and purpose The ability to discriminate between relevant and irrelevant cues, responses and feedback.

Scanning Which would incite task cues, these would enable the robot to identify the relevant cues from irrelevant ones, and interpret the cues received by the use of the next two functions.

Short term memory and *Long term memory* for the purpose of accumulating information received, with the ability to benefit from cognitive awareness; and finally the most important stage of all,

Decision making and problem solving Which is carried out based on the analysis of the acquired information.

Miller's taxonomy illustrates the desire on the part of theorists who typically wish to maintain maximum control over the trainee. It also points to the presence of a mechanistic philosophy which underlies such taxonomies. The trainee is likened to a mechanical device. His ability to make correct decisions and ability to solve problems is largely assumed to be determined by the nature and amount of information available to him and his ability to retain, analyse and select a course of predetermined behaviours.

The adoption of this kind closed approach to learning is not unique to Miller. A large number of theorists and writers on learning and training have subscribed to the principles of the cybernetic and information schools, where the theories concentrate on how information is received, monitored and utilised for the purpose of decision making. Stammer and Patrick (1975) and Duncan and Kelly (1983) liken the way in which feedback can control human performance to the manner in which 'a thermo-stat controls a heating system' (Kenney and Reid, 1986, p.121). The work of writers such as Thomas (1962), Seymour (1968), Wright and Taylor (1970), and Jackson (1984) are examples where interesting developments in the field of electronics, computer and information processing have had influence on an authors perception of the reality of

25

learning. Training is regarded as a means for creating the desired response, albeit intelligently and selectively, from amongst the options available and information which is accessible to the individual trainee.

Learner: controlled or in control?

A chronological review of the theories and writings on the subject of learning indicates the presence of an implicit concern for the degree of control which the learner would have over the learning processes, situation, what needs to be learnt and whether or not the learnt material is transferable. The major assumptions which have been held by theorists and writers concerning the role of the individual in relation to learning have been marked on a continuum (see Figure 2.1).

Concern for	*Information*	*The human*	*Experience and*
behaviour	*processing*	*potential*	*autonomy*
|------------------	|---------------------	|------------------------	|------------------- |

Learner   **Learner in**
controlled   **control**

Figure 2.1   Continuum of position of theorists concerning
the issues of 'learning' and 'control'

The two situations; individual learner as being 'controlled' and being 'in control' of his own learning represent the two extreme ideological positions from which the learner has been dealt with.

Concern for behaviour

One extreme position on the continuum accommodates the likes of Watson (1924) and Pavlov (1927) who were concerned with conditioning and behaviourists such as Skinner (1954; 1965) (neo-behaviourist) and

26

Thorndike (1898) who were mainly interested in the powers of the 'operant' or 'instrumental conditioning'. Such writers, despite the differences in the nature of their work, all showed to a greater or lesser degree, concern for the way people behave. The study of behaviour as an involuntary reflex, as stimulus to specific responses or molar behaviour which connected units of behaviours together, represented concern for what can be done to people. In short, how we can make people behave in a desired way.

Conditioning The most basic and most talked about concept associated with the subject of learning is that of conditioning or shaping behaviour. The reader needs to be reminded that most experiments which were carried out in that era involved , in one way or another, animals in carefully   controlled   conditions. The results obtained were used to explain complex behaviours, such as that of Man. While the Classical theories of conditioning provided the stepping stones towards understanding how animals learn, psychologists soon realised that using simple concepts such as Stimuli-Response can not explain all behaviours, especially the behaviour of Man.

Skinner (1965) based his work on the famous experiments which were originally carried out by Thorndike (the Thorndike Puzzle Box), whereby a cat was placed in a wooden slatted box and was observed in order to see how long it would take before the cat managed to manipulate the mechanism which allowed it to reach the food reward it could see through the slats in the box. Once the cat managed this task it was then placed back in the box and the whole operation was repeated many times. After twenty tries the cat learnt to manipulate the mechanism as soon as it was placed back in the box. The conclusion which was reached was that the actions which had pleasant consequences were more likely to be repeated than those which did not.

The Law of Effect, which was originally introduced by Thorndike, opened up a new horizon for psychologists such as Skinner, who learnt how to 'get the right response' by 'strengthening' and 'weakening' instead of 'stamping in' and 'stamping out' which were used previously by Thorndike. More importantly, Skinner also used the term reinforcement in place of the Law of Effect.

According to Skinner, 'behaviour which is reinforced tends to be repeated, behaviour which is not reinforced tends to die out or be extinguished. To reinforce is to strengthen, so behaviour which is strengthened tends to be repeated' Hardy and Hayes (1979, p.79).

Despite the serious criticism of his work, Skinner should be remembered for his findings that behaviour can be shaped and maintained, by its consequences. Whether the behaviour is positively or negatively reinforced it results in the 'strengthening' of the response. However, should punishment be used as a consequence to a behaviour it weakens the response and the memory of such punishment will result in aversive stimuli.

Reward and punishment The term 'operant conditioning' means operations performed by organisms on a voluntary basis and the term was originally coined by Skinner and is still in use. Skinner used 'reward' and 'punishment' (reinforcements) to shape the behaviour of animals. Each time the desired response was performed food was offered which strengthened the use of such behaviour. While the complexity and sophistication of human beings can not be compared to animals, the concept of reinforcement has implications for many types of learning. Reinforcement provided the educators, trainers, theorists and behaviourists, as a whole, with the opportunity to modify the behaviour of, for example, handicapped children and adults and to achieve positive results in learning more complicated social skills (Gross, 1991).

For trainers, in particular, conditioning and the use of 'reward' and 'punishment' meant that when the correct response was given on the part of the trainee (learner) a reward was offered. For example, "You have done very well" or "Very good" as opposed to "You made a mistake". This will then reinforce the use of correct responses and so motivate them to extend their learning (Kenney and Reid, 1986, p.118).

Although Skinner's ideas have been widely criticised, it is interesting to observe that, it is generally agreed, in so far as reinforcement is concerned, that reward (positive and negative reinforcement) is a much more potent influence on behaviour than punishment both with animals and humans. '.... you can not teach an animal or a person anything new by punishment alone' (Gross,1979, p.61).

Cognitive theorists such as Breakwell et al (1982), Walker (1979) and many others questioned the validity of learning which takes place under conditioning and offered other explanations such as learning the relationships between events, learning 'sets' of behaviour and learning by trial and error, thus indicating the presence of the cognitive processes and their impact on learning.

Thus, it was purported that a single trial learning may not be adequate and attempts on the part of the learner, even with the benefit of supervision, may result in rule learning. This has had important implications for trainers. The abilities of the individual trainee to learn is argued to be dependent upon more than just the presence or absence of reinforcement. The individuals' capability to learn ought to be taken into consideration (Hardy and Hayes, 1979). This has probably been the main contribution to the notion of using IQ tests for assessing the degree of intelligence of trainees and whether or not the trainee has the capability for learning particular skills with different degrees of complexity and difficulty.

Although those who subscribe to behaviourism and cognitive theories with concern for learning as an external process and not necessarily as a function of S-R, but learning as a meaningful concept, made an interesting distinction between short term learning and 'generalised learning skills', they failed to see the individual himself in charge of the learning processes and directly involved in the training activities. For the above theorists learning seems to be concerned with doing things to people. Clearly the people's choice, their willingness, intrinsic motivation and their commitment to learning knowledge, skills, and new attitudes and values is understated. As Jones (1979) remarks;

> The behaviourist position probably owes its pre- eminence in some fields to its clarity and [seemingly] scientific aura. Also, it can point to some concrete demonstrations of its application - as in programmed learning. Those who find it unattractive object to its seemingly non-humanist flavour - for example, the endlessly documented experiments with rats and pigeons (p. 24).

Information processing

The next important phase in the development of learning was marked by the development of radar and automatic weapon systems just after World War ll. The concern with efficiency and control and to a large extent inventing machines which could mostly manage their own operations, drew attention towards self-monitoring devices which could act independently based on the information available to them. A fridge for instance, is equipped with an example of an information processing system which can monitor its own operations. When it senses that a predetermined temperature has been obtained, it will automatically switched off and then on again once the sensor registers the need to once again cool the system. The common principle in the design of all automatic devices, be it a sophisticated radar or a simple toaster, is the notion of the 'feedback loop'.

The increased efficiency and accuracy demonstrated by automated mechanical and electrical devices has inspired writers such as Wiener (1948), Shanon, (1948), Attneave (1959), Annett (1961) and more recently Holloway (1974), Stammers and Patrick (1975) and Duncan and Kelly (1983) to use the above principles in order to improve the performance of and increase control over learning processes. The individual trainees were thought to use information received in the form of feedback from the environment to alter, modify and even change their behaviour. Information constituted the most important component of the system. Thus, people were believed to function like machines with predictable and calculable responses and with a reliable degree of accuracy.

How does it work? The individual receives information through sense organs. Some sensory organs collect information and monitor changes which occur inside the body such as sensations of pain, feelings of hunger, thirst (interceptors). Others gather information from outside the body thus monitoring the external physical environment (exteroceptors). Finally, there are the sensory organs (proprioceptors) which register the feelings of touch (skin) monitor movement, distance (eyes) sounds (ears). In this way the information collected is fed to the brain where already learnt (programmes) courses of action will enable the individual to choose from amongst the courses of actions available to him. For example, if an object is too hot to be lifted with bare hands, it should picked up by using some insulating material or left alone to become cool enough to be picked up by hand. In the words of Stammer and Patrick (1974) 'Such regulation is only possible because of the feedback loop and such a system is therefore considered to be closed-loop and under feedback control' (p.25).

The implication of these discoveries for training people to learn a task are numerous. Especially so, for situations where the learning of tasks and skills are involved. The instructor or trainer's main role is to set up the situation in which the performance of the trainee can be monitored and commented on (feedback) so that the trainee can adjust his response until he gains mastery of that particular skill. The role of the trainer as the provider of feedback for improving the learning and performance of the trainee has received much attention (Adams, 1968; Annett, 1969).

The adoption of the principles of information processing to training placed the trainer in control of the learning situation. It was expected that the trainee, in his role as learner, by following instructions, listening to

30

feedback given and through practice would eventually learn to provide the right response. The trainer's knowledge of the desired performance and the ways in which tasks could be broken down into simple operations (Seymour, 1968) and the shortest route to learning the skills, placed him at the centre of attention and made him almost indispensable. The claim was that 'training time could be shortened considerably by providing practice in recognising and reacting to the stimuli used by those with experience, rather than allowing the learner to work unsupervised and thereby reinforcing less effective habits such as the 'hurt' and 'peck' method' (Kenney and Reid, 1986, p.122).

Learning to use a key board, operating a lathe, driving and other skill-related operations could be explained in that manner. Holloway (1974) uses learning to drive as an example of actions which are controlled by feedback but organised in hierarchical fashion (Stammer and Patrick, 1975, p.40). In order to perform more complex operations a plan for operations of different activities is needed whereby at each stage of carrying out an activity, a set of instructions which are designed to achieve the desired state is available. These stages could be arranged sequentially so that each action provides the basis for the next.

Miller et al (1960), offered the concept of 'test, operation, test and exit', which in its simplest form could explain the behaviour of the rider who coordinates the movements of the bike with the desired direction, makes the necessary adjustments (operates) and sees (test) if it has brought the bike to the desired position, if not the sequence of operation is repeated until the desired state is achieved, and then he stops steering (exit). Accidents could be explained as a situation where unexpectedly a new course of action is required for which the rider has not been prepared or which cannot be put into action as quickly as is necessary (Kay, 1983). The rider suddenly encounters a cat crossing the street. Avoiding a collision, to a large extent will depend on the availability of various programmed and learnt responses, the time spent on choosing the right response and the taking of the action needed before reaching the target.

The value of experience in recognising and dealing with the ways that things can go wrong can only make a difference where an unplanned response is needed to meet the requirement of an unforeseen situation.

Information and managers In the field of management training, managers are taught to become sensitive to the information present in and outside of the work environment, to collect and sift through, analyse and use the necessary information to monitor and control the operations and take action. Effective communication, access to relevant data, the ability and skills on the part of the manager to analyse and convert data to usable properties, and the availability of suitable technology are believed to contribute to the effectiveness of managers.

Of course, in practice things could go wrong. Situations may develop where the model of Man as an information processor may not constitute an adequate metaphor to explain the outcome. For example, let's consider an individual in a managerial position. Since a managers job is far too complex to be preprogrammed for all eventualities and the speed with which he needs to take action and deal with the unexpected constraints and uncertainties, 'it is simply not feasible for him to communicate everything to everyone. He must decide what is to be communicated and to whom, and these decisions will be constrained by his knowledge of others' jobs and his perception of the abilities and knowledge of other people' (Smith et al, 1982, p.117).

With the development of efficient information processing devices some theorists have shown a tendency to liken the efficient employee, operator or even manager to a well programmed computer. In reality, however, the human side of trainees, the differences in their value structures and perceptions, their unique interpretations of events and the unpredictability of the ways in which they deal with similar situations limits the use of humans as machines. More importantly, this approach to training managers and operatives, ignores the potential of people and their need for growth and development.

Human potential

The middle position of the continuum accommodates the wishes of the Humanists, who in contrast with the behaviourists, place emphasis on the whole existential aspect of the learner. The importance given to the value and the potential of the learner and the emphasis placed on the wishes of the individuals for self-development and actualisation is clearly evident in the work of eminent writers such as Rogers (1951) 'Client Centred Therapy'; 'On Becoming a Person' (1967); and 'Encounter Groups' (1970).

Organisation writers concerned with the behaviour of people in the workplace have inevitably been influenced by the findings of the Human Relations School. Writers such as McGregor (1961) and Maslow (1970) are notable examples of those who place greater emphasis on the individual as a learner, the need on his part for development and of course, the motivation which is needed to realise an individual's potential.

MacGregor's Theory X and Y, is a useful analogy which explains the nature of the relationship between the assumptions we hold concerning people and their attitude to work and how this affects people's behaviour, their responses towards us and their orientation to work. This has profound implications for trainers and how they perceive the trainees. For example, if it is assumed that a trainee lacks the potential, drive or interest for learning certain materials or skills, there is a strong likelihood that he will behave accordingly: a self fulfilling philosophy.

Motivation and needs satisfaction   Maslow suggests that there is an ascending hierarchy of needs in operation which determines the level of motivation of an individual to work. According to Maslow, there are five sequentially ordered needs, namely physiological, security, social, self-esteem and self-actualisation. The satisfaction of lower class of needs will create the craving towards satisfying the needs in the higher levels of hierarchy. Once the physiological needs (hunger and thirst), security needs (safer environment), social needs (friendship, recognition and love), and self-esteem (respect, autonomy) are satisfied, the individual will strive towards 'satisfying and realising the needs of one's own potential, more often than not, through the undertaking of challenging works' (Kakabadse, 1987, p.121).

The above theories have created the foundation for a succession of writers to strive towards finding ways of improving individual performance in work organisations. Training and development, therefore, can constitute a major step towards realising the full potential of people at work. In designing a training programme, the trainers are, therefore, expected to give as much consideration to the intrinsic factors such as the need for 'recognition', 'control' and 'affiliation' as the extrinsic factors such as reward, supervision, working conditions and the like. Hertzberg (1968); Locke, (1968); Alderfer (1972); and Nowaday (1979), have stressed the potential of the individual for development and betterment with importance placed on choosing the correct motivator to facilitate and enhance the process of learning, training for a new task or preparing for a more challenging responsibility.

It is believed that the application of the above theories which are designed to 'tap' into the hidden potential of individuals for learning certain skills and knowledge could directly and indirectly result in improved performance and greater productivity on their part.

Nowadays, the expectations from the trainers, in terms of their skills, knowledge and competence for dealing with people, as complex beings, has increased. Trainers are expected to not only possess the relevant knowledge and necessary expertise in the 'task-related' aspects of their job, but also to be able to know exactly what can facilitate and enhance the learning processes involved.

It is evident that as we move away from the behaviourists and the cybernetics' positions, on the suggested continuum of control, the need for allowing the trainee to gain and exercise a greater degree of autonomy over the learning processes becomes increasingly recognised. The authoritarian approaches and styles in training, therefore, need to be replaced by methods which involve more trainee participation .

Tai (1985) in his discussion of current participative learning draws attention to the necessary qualification of the trainer as a 'facilitator'. He maintains that 'If the trainer is perceived by the participants (trainees) as a person having genuiness, empathy and respect for others, he is likely be successful in facilitating learning groups' (p.15).

Participation in learning activities tends to integrate the learner into the social organisation of the learning situation. The learner experiences the learning processes as they occur and will share his views concerning what is to be learnt and how it should be learnt with others. The role of the trainer, therefore, should be a facilititive one which does not call for exercising unnecessary control. The trainer ought to act as a guide with the intention of directing learners towards their learning objectives, whilst allowing the learner to experience the whole affair as a participant.

Experience and autonomy

In contrast with the orthodox models of learning, one which stipulates the need for structured learning and controlled situations, with the trainer in complete control and the learner as playing a merely passive role, 'learning by doing' and 'experience' sees the role of the individual learner as that of the designer and planner of his own learning programme. The concept of 'learning by doing' is not something new. As Pedler (1983) succinctly remarks, 'we may all agree that learning by doing is in many forms, nothing very new. It is one of the primary forces of evolution, and has accompanied mankind since long before our ancestors came down from the trees' (p.10).

In fact it is not the 'doing' itself which is of so much interest but the very stand from which the learner, the task, the learning situation and the role of the trainer and educator are viewed. It is the realistic underlying philosophy of this approach to learning and training which has made it novel, interesting and successful. To begin with, it is believed that learning situations should be sequenced in such a way that learners with many different styles of learning can benefit from it, while being enabled 'to [be integrated] into a meaningful whole (Bramely, 1990, p.19).

What makes this approach to learning a realistic one is that it is not just the differences in cognition amongst the learners which is taken into consideration, but that people, based on their overall life experiences, the demands with which people are faced and the successful ways in which they interact with others and their environment, will develop a set of preferences for particular ways of learning (Kolb et al 1974).

Learning cycle The above authors suggest that learning should be viewed as a cycle comprised of four distinct stages, which explain how the learning takes place sequentially. The thesis is based on their appealing argument that whatever happens to an individual, albeit negative or positive, forms a 'concrete experience' which becomes the subject of the subsequent 'observation' or 'reflection'. The learning which has taken place will then be put into a framework which could be 'generalised' to future situations. The concepts, abstracts and theories which have been developed will then be utilised for testing new reality 'situations'. More importantly, it is suggested that for some individuals, concrete experience may be of more concern than observation and reflection.

Thus, the notion of individual preferences has emerged. Keenoy and Reid (1986) explain, 'A mathetician might give preference to abstract concepts, while a manager might have greater concern for concrete experience and the active participation of ideas' (p.127). Kolb, Rubin and McIntyre (1974) have developed a learning style inventory, comprised of a questionnaire which enables the learner to identify their most preferred style of learning. The 'converger', 'diverger', 'assimilator' and 'accommodator' have been described as the four approaches to learning. The above classification of learners is based on the rationale that while the individuals show preference for one specific style of learning more than others, for example, learning by 'concrete experience', they are quite capable of adopting other approaches in their learning process. For example, the individual with a preference for 'assimilation' is likely to combine abstract conceptualisation and reflective observation and, therefore, his strength would be in inductive reasoning and creating theoretical models. The knowledge of a learners preferred 'styles' assists the trainer or educator to design a more effective learning situation as well as providing greater awareness on the part of the learner as to 'why I learn the way I do' and 'how I am inclined to approach learning situations and activities, as the whole'.

Kolb's notion of the 'learning cycle' has been criticised by many on the grounds that it tends to typify the individual learner as, diverger, converger, assimilator and accommodator, and pays less attention to the learning approaches themselves.

Hanoy and Mumford (1982) argue that learning ought to be viewed as 'a process which can best be based on the provision of consequences that are rewarding'. They further argue that 'we have built our views of the learning styles, and the questionnaire, around recognisable statements of managerial behaviour' (p.4).

The learning styles identified by Harvey and Mumford are, 'Activist, who involve themselves fully and without bias in new experiences; Reflector, who stands back to ponder on what has been experienced and observes them from many different perspectives; Theorists, who adapt and integrate observation into complex but logically sound theories; and finally, Pragmatists, who are keen on trying ideas, theories and techniques to see if they work in practice' (1982, P.17).

Other writers, especially those concerned with management education and training, have designed other learning inventory tests which are intended to assist the trainers to find out more about the likes and dislikes of the trainees, thus arguing that self awareness, if not the key, is one of the most essential factors towards effective learning, and development.

Margerison and McCann (1984), interviewed many managers on their work performances and established the individual preferences for a specific kind of work. It can be concluded, with a certain degree of plausibility, that the differences in preferences shown by the individuals for the kind of job that they like to do, is also indicative of their preferences towards learning specific skills and knowledge which they have found to be most useful in terms of furthering their learning interests and career in that direction.

Often, the cognitive abilities and preferences which form the cognitive map of the individual learner is used to indicate their preferred styles of learning. In agreement with Harvey and Mumford (1982), 'while such Inventory Tests are of interest, it is more useful to identify how behaviour can be modified rather than to explain the background to the behaviour' (p.5).

What are the implications of this approach to realising effective transfer? It would be simplistic to think that, one specific style, be it reflector, theorist or pragmatist, could make the individual more effective. In agreement with Kennedy and Reid (1986) it would seem that the ability to use all four styles is of particular advantage. More importantly, is that, the learner should not be viewed in isolation from the actual work environment. Indeed, it is feasible, as it has been observed in a variety of work organisations by Richardson and Bennett (1984), that the unique cultural forces within an organisation may act as a barrier, thus encouraging or discouraging the learning or adoption of a specific style of learning. As it will be shown in later discussions, the invisible course of social learning processes, present in any workplace, which the new employee - a learner - is expected to complete, tends to act either as facilitator or inhibitor, thus enabling or impeding the processes of learning. The awareness on the part of the learner of his own approach to learning, the realisation that there are cultural forces in the workplace that regulate people's behaviour and the identification of the preferred style which is legitimised by the organisation, is crucial to the individuals' overall effectiveness, development and success in their job.

As we move further away from classical learning theories, the number of supporters of the contemporary views who feel that learning should be a 'meaningful' experience, and that learners ought to be placed in charge of their own learning increases. When it comes to describing a role for trainers, the common denominator amongst these innovative learning conceptualisations is that the trainers should not perceive their role as being in 'control' of learning activities. Equally, it is expected that the learners contribute to the learning process by becoming aware of their own tendencies, preferences and knowledge of what is best suited to their actual needs. Kenney and Reid (1986) assert, 'The emphasis has moved away from activities largely controlled by the trainer, to learning processes and where possible to self-directed and self-managed learning, using the opportunities provided by new technology such as computer assisted programmemes' (p.129). The concept of 'contract' learning originally offered by Knowles (1975), which attempts to further integrate the learner and organisation in order to improve the transfer of the learnt knowledge and skills, has now gathered wide spread support by subscribers to adult-learning.

When the success that 'action learning' has recently had in realising effective learning for managers and practitioners in industry is considered, it is almost inevitable to see the implicit concern of the contempary theorists and writers involved to move towards an improved degree of effective learning and its transfer.

What is even more exciting about 'experimental-learning' is its underlying premise that at the end of the day, it is the performance in the organisational context which should be the ultimate concern. Here, it is worth reiterating that learning by itself should not become the sole concern for trainers and practitioners. Indeed it should be the consequences of such cognetive processes, observed in terms of changes in behaviour, attitude and performance of the trainee on the job within the workplace which ought to become the focus. The organisation in its entirety should be considered as a complex and dynamic learning situation in which the people and the work-related activities inevitably affect the learnt material in their likely observable consequences, and the realisation and occurance of the expected transfer.

To view learning as an isolated event which begins with trainees entering the training centre and ends when the trainees leave with certificates in their hands, is incongruent with the reality of the individual learner as an organisational member and active decision maker who is concerned with his or her own development.

The question, why is it that as we get closer to the actual workplace the more effective our training results become? may be answered by emphasising that learning as a process should include the learner, the trainer, the learning situation (either on or off-the job), the organisation of the workplace, both in the social and task-related aspects of its operation.

Useful concepts for trainers

A selection of topics which are believed to be of particular interest to practitioners and training specialists are included here. The aim is to enable the reader to approach the task of designing a learning situation more confidently, while realising the role and influence of the forgone theories on the formation of such practical aids for the trainers. The rationale behind employing this strategy is that, the discussion so far has been concerned with providing an overall perspective which could encompass most learning related theories, concepts and relevant issues. While this is certainly beneficial, particularly to scholars and training specialists, the practitioner who may find themselves in the position of designing a training programme may require practical steps which could be realistically used in the design of learning situations and be incorporated into the training programmes.

To achieve this objective, a selection of useful concepts, namely principles of learning, knowledge of learning, levels of learning, learning curves, social and technical learning and lastly how to design reality into the learning situation, will be briefly discussed. The reader who is already familiar with these concepts may skip this section and join us at the beginning of Chapter Three where the significance of the methods of training for effective transfer are discussed.

The application of learning theories

Since learning has always been and remains an inseparable part of any training activity, this has led to the formation of the belief, in certain quarters, that training should be equated with learning (Blumfield & Holland, 1971). This association, however, is not unusual because without learning no training activity can realistically be expected to take place. As shown earlier, we owe our present understanding of how learning takes place mainly to psychologists who through observation and much experimentation have developed what is known as the 'principles of learning'. It is, nevertheless, important to remember that as Miner (1969) points out, 'our knowledge regarding the specific applications of these principles is unfortunately far from complete. Most of these principles were developed originally within the psychological laboratories, often as a result of work with animals, although subsequent studies have been extended to the human sphere, research has not always been conducted in an industrial setting' (p.207).

This imbalance, has now largely been rectified, especially with the works of writers on organisational development and those who have been particularly concerned with management training development in work organisations (Golembuski, 1976).

As O'Connell (1973) has discovered, there is some degree of similarity present between the teacher-pupil role and that of the supervisor-subordinate roles. He points out the significance of the leader's role (as trainer) in determining the pupils degree of experienced success. Views concerning the role of educators and their relationship with the learner are changing from structured learning processes to self-directed and autonomous ones (Candy, 1991), and this is also the case in the field of training and development. Within the sphere of training for organisational effectiveness, a similar trend is noticeable. The notion of 'learning to learn' is becoming the focus. Yet, it is of the utmost importance for the reader to realise that as Candy (1991) suggests major 'principles derived from various learning theories and findings from experimental research, have remained the same'. Recent research has demonstrated the extent of their impact on learning processes and how important it is for trainers to be aware of these principles and incorporate them in the design of their training - formal and informal programmemes.

A caution, however, needs to be given. Trainers ought to assess for themselves the usefulness and relevance of each classification (taxonomy) and principle offered for use in a particular learning situation. Bearing in mind that the individual differences in terms of cognitive capabilities, the nature of the task and that the actual work situation where training is expected to pay off, are all inherently diverse, trainers should view their role as a 'facilitator' of learning processes and regard the principles of learning as aids and means to and not the ends for, increasing the effectiveness of learning situations.

Major principles

Following the work of Shivers (1980), the following principles have been observed to be regarded as the most significant, by trainers, for accelerating the learning processes in a training situation.

Motivation

In a learning situation, whether it concerns the acquisition of knowledge and skills for operatives or the modification and attainment of new behaviours at managerial level, motivation can play a significant part towards accelerating the learning processes. In the words of Davies, 'It is probably a mistake to think of motivation as a necessary prerequisite for learning. A more useful way of thinking about this force is to regard motivation as a general willingness to enter into a learning situation' (1971, p.150).

As a subject, especially in the field of organisational psychology, it is probably the most talked about concept, which unfortunately is viewed by some practitioners and managers as the sole solution to the problem of low productivity and inferior standards of performance.

The reason for the abundance of theories in this field, often of a contradictory nature, can be attributed to the fact that there is no comprehensive framework which encompasses all human activities (Smith et al, 1982). For our purpose, the first step for a trainer is to ensure that an individual's ability and will to learn is not taken for granted when assessing training needs and using this assessment in planning training and development.

Does the trainee, operative or manager, possess the necessary abilities or skills to learn a task or concept? Is the training group homogeneous in terms of the capability of its individual members to understand the task they are asked to do or, is it the case that some members tend to be 'quicker' to grasp the new ideas than others? Unfortunately most trainers in industry start with the assumption that so long as trainees form a group, their social and interpersonal needs are taken care of. Not many have realised that the satisfaction of social needs can act as a powerful incentive for improved learning.

Interpersonal needs Within the social setting of the learning situation, trainees with different degrees of interpersonal needs, the need for 'achievement', the need for 'power' (control) and the need for 'affiliation' (McClelland 1961) participate in group and learning activities. While, group membership satisfies the 'affiliation' needs of the trainees, their desire for a higher degree of autonomy and control should not be neglected by the trainers. Trainers who can identify these social needs may be able to use them as useful socio-psychological aids to motivate the participant trainees in subtle and indirect ways. For example, in a training centre, it was observed that both in management and operative training the inclusion of learning activities and exercises which resulted in a sense of achievement and fulfilment on the part of the trainees, acted as motivation for greater involvement in learning activities.

Placing the trainees in groups, as a member of a 'learning committees' not only results in the satisfaction of 'affiliation' needs, but also enables them to identify with one or more of their fellow trainees who happen to share a place 'in the same boat'.

On a middle management training course, it was observed that attempts were being made by trainers to persuade the participants to take charge of the activities in the learning situation. Later it was discovered that this policy had been perceived as one of the 'most encouraging aspects of the training programme' by the trainee participants involved.

Satisfiers and dissatisfiers The implications of the two factor theory of motivation, offered by Hertzberg et al, (1959), is an equally important concept for a trainer as it is for a manager in charge of a work organisation. First the trainer has to identify the 'dissatisfiers', the elements present in the learning situation which are likely to create dissatisfaction for the trainees, and then employ a strategy to either eliminate them or at least to minimise their harmful effects on the trainees.

The importance of the physical condition of the learning environment itself, is often taken for granted by trainers. It is nowadays recognised that comfortable working conditions are conducive to effective learning. The use of suitable learning aids such as overheads, video material and other visual aids can often provide the motivation necessary to learn the most difficult of concepts.

Also, it is of the utmost importance for trainers and instructors to correctly identify what initiates and facilitates learning processes. Hertzberg refers to this group of motivators as 'satisfiers'. The first step to be taken towards motivating trainees is to identify 'how much they already know' and 'what they are capable of'.

The use of 'Assessment Tests' for identifying how much trainees already know and what they are capable of, is becoming increasingly popular, especially in the sphere of management development training.

The use of the 'Self-Inventory Tests' for the identification of the learning styles (Honey and Mumford, 1982) of the trainee participants is an excellent example of how greater self awareness can direct the individual learner towards better achievement of the identified learning objectives.

Willingness to learn Another important question which needs to be asked is; Is there sufficient 'will' or 'interest' in the individual to continue to learn what is expected of him or her ? Kenney and Reid (1986) argue that in the same way that a horse can be taken to the water but can not be forced to drink it, 'people learn if they accept the need for training and are committed to it'(p.130).

The problem usually faced is how to measure commitment in an individual trainee. While there is no easy or fast answer to this question, experienced trainers have reported that the trainee's approach to learning, the rate of attention paid to the workshop activities, the regular attendance of training sessions, the degree of concentration shown to the subjects and the presentation of the output, all provide subtle clues or indicators for the trainer to assess the 'will' and 'commitment', on the part of the trainee.

Most theorists believe that intrinsic motivation is undoubtedly the most powerful means towards learning and development, as a whole, though, as Shiver (1980) suggests the importance of extrinsic factors, such as the learning condition itself, shouldn't be ruled out.

Basically, the theories of motivation point out the presence of 'needs' such as physiological, safety, social, ego, self esteem and self actualisation (Maslow, 1970) which once they have been sufficiently satisfied, could motivate the individual or group concerned towards improved performance and accelerated learning. The satisfaction of the interpersonal needs, greater participation on the part of the trainee, increased responsibility for self-need analysis, monitoring and planning the training activities and its outcome by the individual learners themselves, are some of the subtle but powerful motivators in the armoury of the experienced trainer.

Expectation and the invested effort For the serious trainer, it is vital to understand what is the main motivation for the trainee to join a particular training programme.   What are the trainee's short or long term expectations from the training programme? It is often the expectation of individual trainee from the outcome of a training programme, whether the actual outcome will meet their expectations or not, that acts as motivator for them to be engaged in a particular training activity. According to Vroom's (1964) 'expectancy theory', three distinct phases of motivation to undertake an activity are identifiable. The expectancy theory is about how people make decisions which can also be applied to learning situations. It can therefore be argued that the 'efforts' which an individual trainee invests in learning an activity is linked to his expectations of the outcome. This could be the first or even second level outcome.

For example, first the effort is linked to an expectation. "If I learn I will become more productive". The second stage links the target to an outcome. "An improved performance on my part, may result in future promotion".   The third stage consists of an evaluation of outcome; "Promotion means an increase in remuneration",. The description of what the desired outcome should be, largely depends on the individual's perception and his subjective preferences for the likely outcome of his effort (Smith et al, 1982).

What should be remembered by trainers and educators is that there is a range of choices to be made by the trainee. The individual trainee 'is influenced by how he thinks these behaviours are rewarded' (kakabadse et al 1987 p.28).

Designing a learning situation with the reality of the work organisation in mind and relating the knowledge, skills and attitudes and behaviours to be learnt to an outcome which is realistic and meaningful to the individual trainee constitutes the first major step towards motivating the trainees involved. This undoubtedly increases the probability that positive transfer will take place.

Knowledge of the result

It is often observed that periodical evaluation exercises are undertaken by trainers with the intention of assessing the extent to which the individual trainee has acquired certain skills, knowledge or attitudes. But the results are rarely communicated to the trainees themselves. Those writers such as McGhee and Thayer (1961), Annett (1969) and Stammer and Patrick (1975) who strongly believe in the value of providing regular 'feedback' to trainees, emphasise that knowledge of the result is a significant principle in learning. It is suggested that so long as the learner or trainee is aware of his progress in relation to specific objectives (his target), his progress will be accelerated.

Holding (1965) provides a simple classification of the knowledge of results, intrinsic or extrinsic. Knowledge of result is said to be extrinsic when it is provided externally. For example, a comment made by the instructor (extrinsic) which tells the individual how well or poorly he is doing. It is intrinsic when the individual becomes aware of his own rate of progress by learning to monitor his performance against a set target. Both intrinsic and extrinsic types of feedback provide valuable aids for trainers to accelerate the learning process. In the same way, building autonomy and feedback systems into a job can lead to the motivation of the employee concerned and an improvement in his performance as a result.

Designing a learning situation with a built-in procedure for carrying out self monitoring and evaluation of the progress made in relation to the target objectives, can provide the necessary feedback and hence motivation for the learner to achieve the training objective. It must be born in mind that while provision of relevant information to the trainees and improving communication with them are important, it is the way in which trainees are provided with the above which determines the positive or negative notion of the reward.

If the trainee views the feedback as a positive action on the part of the trainer, it is more likely that feedback, as argued by Kenney and Reid (1986) will act as a 'reinforcement'. However, should the trainee be critically informed of how badly he is doing, whether it is done intentionally or unintentionally, there is a chance that his self-esteem will be impaired by receiving negative feedback, thus having negative effect on his performance. In this case because the knowledge of the result has been viewed as punishment, the provision of feedback may be followed by demotivation or a loss of interest on the part of the receiver, the trainee involved.

The role of the trainer, as a communicator, needs to be taken much more seriously, especially where the training consists of a great deal of social learning input. Also, the procedure by which the trainee is provided with knowledge of his results, especially where his learning capability and progress are concerned, needs to have particular attention paid to it.

First, as far as possible, trainees should be allowed to monitor their own progress and the training materials which are provided should be 'user friendly'.

Secondly, a point which is not usually highlighted in textbooks, but which in practice has proven to be of importance, is the accurate assessment of the exact time when the trainee should be provided with the knowledge of results. When a programme of learning is designed for a particular task, specific times for providing the trainee with knowledge of what he has achieved should be incorporated into the schedule. In essence, the 'timing' of when to provide feedback should not be indiscriminate or used solely in order to boost the self esteem of the learner. Having said that, it is equally as important, and almost crucial that, should a trainee ask for feedback on how he has been performing, the trainer provides him with knowledge of what he has actually achieved rather than what he was expected to have achieved.

Learning curve

Learning Curve can be used to measure the rate of progress made by the learner and can be of some value to both the trainer and trainee. Typically a curve is used to plot the progress of the individual in learning or performing a task in terms of the number of tries, efforts or times taken to accomplish that activity. The curve consists of a vertical axis on which what percentage of the performance was a correct response, is measured and marked, and the horizontal axis which demonstrates the number of tries. Bass and Vaughn (1966) distinguish between three types, namely the *negative accelerated, positive accelerated* and well known *plateau state* learning curve.

The negative accelerated describes a situation whereby the initial rate of learning had been much greater in the early stages and which gradually slowed down as time passed.

In the case of positive accelerated learning situations, the learner may find the process of learning a specific material, skill or even a behavioural

45

change initially difficult, probably because the learner's past preparation [has been] insufficient or the initial motivation is low' (Glueck, 1974). Thus initial slow progress will gradually be followed by a faster rate in subsequent trials.

The state of 'plateau' is experienced when for some reason progress has halted but may begin to accelerate again after a period of almost 'unlearning'. In fact, motivation is often found to be a major issue in the occurrence of 'plateaux' and thus joint attempts between the trainer and trainee to plot the progress made on a learning curve will provide both the trainee and trainer with the information necessary to adjust his performance and eventually overcome the temporary lack of progress.

The knowledge of results obtained in this way provides essential feedback for the trainee as to how well he is doing, as well as providing him with an objective measure with which to plan his own learning programme and periodically adjust the content, structure and/or amount of time allocated to each learning activity.

Other useful principles such as 'whole learning' as opposed to 'part learning', 'learning motor skills' as opposed to 'cognitive learning' and 'reinforcement' are amongst the most notable recommendations which are made by writers such as Davies (1971) and Shiver (1980). The argument put forward is that the use of such principles in a training situation could accelerate the learning processes and thus contribute to the effectiveness of the training.

Discussions concerning the use of 'reinforcement' can be found in the previous section where the issue of conditioning was dealt with. Motor skill learning and whole learning, social and technical learning are discussed below.

Hierarchy of learning

Certainly, Gagne's (1970) taxonomy, is one of the most interesting and influential typologies available in the field of learning and one which has special relevance for the debate on training and transfer. Unlike Miller's (1967) taxonomy which fails to directly relate the different training methods to each of the proposed learning categories, Gagne's typology offers the novel notion of 'discreet' learning. He suggests that in order to have an effective learning instruction the programme should be tailor made to the needs of each identified type of learning.

Gagne's reasons for distinguishing between various learning types include, first of all, the claim that to some extent the identified variables

46

tend to affect the process of learning and the acquisition of skills and knowledge.

Secondly, it is suggested that more emphasis ought to be placed on the hierarchical nature of the learning types. He proposes an eight variables learning category which appears to form a hierarchy in terms of the learning complexity involved. These are;-

Signal learning Gagne argues that the most basic and rudimentary type of learning is signal learning. 'The individual learns to make a general diffuse response to a signal' (Stammer and Patrick, 1975, p.50).

Gagne's notion of signal learning is in line with Pavlov's (1849-1936) experiments with dogs.

Classical conditioning Pavlov a Russian psychologist introduced his concept early in 1909. He was primarily concerned with measuring the flow of saliva in dogs as a part of his study of digestive glands. He observed that when the meat is placed in the mouth of the animal, naturally the saliva began to flow.

It was noted that, the dog salivated (unconditioned response) each time it heard the sound of the bell. The bell's sound was used as a signal (neutral stimuli) to initiate salvation even when no meat was offered to the dog. Pavlov used signal learning, a somewhat primitive concept, to make the generalisation that, 'all behaviours were the result of reflex actions to certain stimuli which could either be external such as visual, oral, tactile or internal changes in the body mechanism due to hunger, thirst, fatigue and so on' (O,Connell, 1973, p.19).

Gagne refers to signal learning as specific events which could be used as a form of 'conditioned' or 'unconditioned' stimuli. This in turn can be utilised in training to initiate a general and diffuse response to signals received.

Stimuli-Response learning

The Stimuli-Response (S-R) type of learning, advocated by Gagne, refers to a higher order learning concept in which 'the learner acquires a precise response to a discriminated stimuli' (Stammers and Patrick, 1975, p.50).

S-R theories of learning emanate from the conditioning experiments which were originally developed by Pavlov (1927). Indeed, as Luthans (1981), asserts since the era of conditioning experiments 'many psychologists have attempted to classically condition almost everything from the flat worm to human beings'(p.230). Bass and Vaughn (1966) state;

> In all probability, any response in an organism's behavioural repertoire can be conditioned if an unconditioned stimulus can be found that regularly produces the response and if this unconditioned stimulus can be paired in training with a conditioned stimulus (p.15).

Nevertheless, the theoretical possibility of conditioning represents only 'a very small part of the total human being' (Luthans, 1981, p.237).

Skinner (1954) further introduced the effect of the environment on learning and more importantly *operant conditioning*, where learning occurs as a consequence of specific behaviour. Gagne has successfully distinguished between the first and the latter types of learning on the basis that signal learning leads to involuntary responses whereas the latter, S-R learning, is carried out under voluntary control.

Chaining Gagne believes that chaining or *several learning* occurs when a chain of stimuli and responses are formed. Originally the conditions under which this kind of learnings were produced was discovered by Skinner. Basically, the chaining type of learning falls into the cognitive category of learning theories. According to Skinner and Tolman's experimentations, however, the response to a particular stimulus results from the learning process. Thus, by connecting a few S-Rs in a learning situation, the response from one action can be used as a stimulus for the next one. It has been critically argued that 'chaining' results in learning but not a great deal of understanding (O,Connell, 1973).

Verbal association This form of learning is seen as a sub-variety of chaining. It is the learning of the chains of S-Rs which are of a verbal nature. Although this condition resembles those which are used to initiate other 'motor changes'(i.e. non-verbal activities), nevertheless, as Gagne has aptly asserted, the fact that language itself is an exclusive attribute of human beings makes this type of learning an empirical one, simply because internal links may be selected from the individuals previously learnt repertoire of language (Stammer and Patrick, 1975).

Discriminatory learning Technically the term discrimination has much broader meanings. 'When applied to learning, discrimination is essentially opposite to generalisation' (Luthans, 1981, p.247). This type of learning refers to the ability to or the acquisition of the capability to distinguish amongst various numbers of sets of stimuli. Gagne uses the familiar task of learning to name the letters of the alphabet as an example of multi-discriminatory-learning.

Harlow's (1949) experimentations with monkeys is a notable example of this kind of learning. In his 'learning set' he introduced the monkeys to blocks of different shapes and then they were expected to discriminate between, for example, the triangular shaped blocks if the base was painted yellow, or a circular shaped block if the base was painted green.

In our daily activities we discriminate between different stimuli. For instance, 'we quickly learn to discriminate between a red and a green light' (O,Connell, 1973, p.21).

Concept learning Usually occurs when a learner acquires the capacity to make a common response to a class of stimuli that may be widely different from each other in physical appearance. For example, the concept of *circle* would be an instance of a *concrete* concept which once learnt can be applied to recognise all objects with a circular shape. Gagne argues that concrete concepts are distinguished from other types of learning by the very fact that they are rule determined.

Rule learning In its simplest term, rule learning can be viewed as a 'chain of two or more concepts' (Stammer and Patrick, 1975, p.51). Gagne, in his debate concerning the hierarchy of learning types ascertains that the acquisition of the rule 'round things roll' requires the pre-acquisition of the learning of at least two other concrete concepts. First learning, what is 'round' and second how rolling takes place.

Problem solving Prerequisite to this is believed to be the presence of the internal processes usually referred to as 'thinking'. Gagne believes that problem solving is the highest form of learning type. He contends that problem solving is essentially nothing but the application of rules which leads to the discovery of higher order rules. Gagne argues that, because of the hierarchical nature of learning, problem solving cannot occur unless other types of learning such as discrimination, concept and rule learning has already been completed. The capability to discover higher-rules is regarded by Gagne as problem solving.

A notable example of the application of Gagne's taxonomy is reported by Lawson (1974). Lawson gives examples of a management problem solving task-learning hierarchy in which the activities necessary for problem solving (in a training programme) and the learning sequences are analysed and diagramed in their order of priority. The trainee, therefore, is expected to follow the order in which learning types occur and proceed upwards towards the hierarchy of training activities.

It must, however, be noted that one taxonomy alone can not be applied independently as an entirely adequate concept to effectively design and construct different learning situations. Having said that, it is equally important to remember that Gagne's concept of hierarchical learning types is generally regarded as particularly useful because the distinction is made between two major functions in training; the task analysis and training design. 'The training sequence is suggested by the types of learning which are isolated during the task analysis' (Stammer and Patrick, 1975, p.83).

Levels of learning

This and Lippit (1966) carried out an exhaustive review of the literature on training and confidently concluded that learning can be seen to take place along a continuum in relation to the complexity of the materials that have to be learnt for a particular task. Further, they argued that it is possible to isolate various distinct levels of learning along the proposed continuum.

At the simplest level they identify those learning activities which concern the acquisition of skills of *motor response* such as memorisation and simple conditioning.

Learning at the second level concerns the learning activities which have to be modified or slightly changed if they are to be used in different environments. For instance, a change from operating an old machine to a new one. This type of learning could be viewed as an *up grading* of an already acquired skill.

The third level, as argued by This and Lippit (1966), encapsulates the range of more *complex learning* activities. For example, learning how to find more meanings in seemingly isolated parts and initiating activities which aim towards the acquisition of interpersonal skills.

Finally, the most complex level of learning is described as those types of learning activities which require partial or complete changes in attitude on the part of the learner. For example, the learning of new values, learning a new style of leadership or adopting a new managerial philosophy.

The first two simpler levels of learning proposed by This and Lippit, resemble the kinds of learning categories which normally concerns the acquisition of skills or knowledge required for performing manual work and thus are more relevant to the design of operative training programmes. The latter two categories tend to be more related to managerial jobs where the training mainly concerns the acquisition of knowledge and skills for initiating change in order to enable the trainees to achieve personal development.

Five point scale

Davies (1971) devised a novel scheme consisting of a five point scale which was 'used successfully on a large scale task analysis of a complete RAF Trade'(p.46). According to Davis a taxonomy consists of five categories of tasks namely; Signal Task, Procedural Task, Simple Discriminatory Task, Complex Discriminatory Task and finally, Diagnostic or Problem Solving Task are identifiable. These stages in learning correspond to the 'simple' and 'complex' categories of learning offered by This and Lippit (1966) which seem to be largely influenced by Gagne's original concept of an hierarchy of learning types discussed in some detail earlier.

Task-related learning and transfer

Training specialists, practitioners and even managers in both the private and public sectors are all basically concerned with effective training. The term effective training, however, automatically implies that whatever knowledge and skills (mostly task-related) have been acquired in a learning situation should be totally, without any loss, deployed to the actual work situation. A reasonable expectation, which has, by and large, formed the basis for justifying the expenses associated with training and re-training.

As shown here, the concern, quite correctly, should be with effective learning and the understanding of the different theories, views, concepts, principles and typologies available which may act as aids for trainers to facilitate or accelerate learning.

However, it must be remembered that, traditionally most learning processes in which the trainee is actively engaged are primarily designed to take account of his task-related needs, a point, so obvious that it has been taken for granted for such a long time. For example, individual X needs to learn how to carry out a task, be it driving a car, drilling holes in sheets of glass, welding pipes, repairing micro-computers, planning

51

projects or the like. It could also be the case that our trainee X is not new to the task at all and may only require some up grading or up dating of his present knowledge and skills. Assuming that the need for individual X to undertake learning or re-learning a particular task has been carefully considered in the first place and is thought to be necessary, a training programme of some sort will be designed and the trainee will be subjected to various learning activities which are aimed at enabling him to perform the task effectively.

The above scenario is by no mean uncommon. In most situations, following a typical standard procedure, first the training needs of the individual concerned are analysed. Then training as a viable course of action to reduced the perceived gap between the individual's present and desired level of performance will be chosen.

Thus to continue, the learning theories and taxonomies available and the discoveries made throughout decades of research based on working with animals (experimental studies), the observations made and the accounts provided by a succession of trainers, writers and practitioners, all point towards the importance of understanding how learning processes take place and then finding ways of facilitating and accelerating such processes.

Such debates, especially those which evolve around learning and training typically end with a short discussion on transfer in which concepts such as 'positive', 'negative' 'horizontal', 'vertical' and 'conditioning' are briefly discussed to demonstrate how much of the acquired knowledge and skills is transferred to the actual workplace. Throughout, and this is a point of great importance, such discussion usually evolves around how the teaching can be done effectively. The stress is predominantly placed on how to make people do something or how to change their behaviours or attitudes.

The emphasis, whether at training centres or in learning situations within or outside of the workplace environment, is usually placed on enabling the individuals and groups to perform a task. Quite naturally when things go wrong and the trainee has not been able to demonstrate on the job what he had learnt, the typical trainer, educator or specialist tends to retrace the route of the course back to the beginning where the training needs were identified and learning strategies were adopted. This ritual is usually carried out in order to establish what has gone wrong.

Central to the theoretical premises on which this book is based, is that the present (above) approach to the analysis of the transfer of training is not adequate, simply because;

a) it does not take into account all the learning (including social learning processes) which usually takes place in the training situation and on the job

in the workplace itself. And that;
b) some of the these social learning processes may have an undoing effect on the task-related learning and the process of transfer as the whole. Sometimes exerting an irreversible influence on the acquisition process and/or the transfer of that knowledge and skills to the workplace.

While the direct relevance and relationship between learning concepts, training and ultimately the subject of transfer is plausible enough to be accepted, it is envisaged that the explanation for slow learning, low productivity or ineffective performance and a low amount of transfer after the completion of the learning programme, often has something to do with the kind of social learning processes which may not have been given much thought when a training programme is designed.

Let's think of the kind of knowledge and skills which almost all trainees, regardless of the kind of job which they do, need to possess once the training programme is over. The answer to this question lies primarily in the organisation itself, where the consequences of learning and training are expected to be realised and interestingly and ironically, where the effectiveness of the learning is evaluated.

In essence, the subtle learning processes to which each of us as an organisational member is subjected on a daily basis, our previous knowledge of the cultural and social expectations of colleagues, peers and supervisors, and the range of people-related skills, of an implicit or explicit nature, which are needed to remain effective as a member of the organisation, ought to be addressed and considered as seriously as the task-related aspects of training are.

While writers such as Hazes et al (1983), Richards and Bennett (1984) and Handy (1985) drew attention to the inescapable influence of the organisational processes and their effects on learning. The writers who have specifically dealt with transfer do not extend the debate to the dynamic context of the social and technical reality of the workplace and their interaction and influence on the amount of transfer which is expected to occur.

The observations made in industry by the author, and the reports and the comments which have been made by practitioners, training specialists together with actual accounts reported by trainees, operatives and trainee managers, all point to this simple yet taken for granted issue that often the main reason that training is not transferred is not because effective learning has not taken place, but because the learner or trainee has been prohibited, by his colleagues, peers, bosses and even clients of the organisation, either formally or informally, from displaying the knowledge and skills which he had acquired.

There are a host of organisational factors which inevitably and universally affect the individual trainee's perception, his approach to performing a task, his attitude to others, his orientation towards organisational development and which ultimately in a cumulative manner influence and affect the degree of effective transfer which is experienced.

Conclusion

In this chapter, the overal aim has been to examine the development of learning schools, theories and concepts which are relevant to and are utilised for achieving effective training. In doing so, stress has been placed on the ways in which it can be possible for trainers and educators to facilitate, and accelerate, the learning processes necessary for effective transfer.

It is also argued that the present task-related orientation to training and transfer, while necessary, may not be adequate. The questions raised, were intended to point out the inadequacies of the contemporary approach to the issue of transfer, as well as providing clues as to what ought to be done.

Understanding transfer, amongst other things, requires attention being paid to the training methods used to impart knowledge to the trainees. The methods which are available to trainers, also have implications for the extent and nature of the social learning processes and effective transfer. These and other relevant issues will be introduced and dealt with in some detail in Chapter Three.

3 Training methods and transfer

Introduction

In deciding what methods and approaches should be employed for implementing a training programme, training experts and practitioners consider a myriad of factors; the one factor which is given the least consideration is the potential of each method for the realisation of effective transfer.

Why? Simply because transfer has hitherto been viewed as an extension of the learning processes whose occurrence, or lack of it, can only realistically be assessed or determined after the completion of a training programme; when the trainee attempts to put the learnt knowledge and skills into use on the job in the actual workplace. Those who seriously give consideration to whether or not a training method is going to lead to a successful outcome, more often than not tend to focus on the task-related aspects of the learning which the trainee is expected to transfer from the training situation into the actual job context.

Therefore, even when the issue of transfer is seriously considered, it is usually the 'transfer of learning' rather than the 'transfer of training' which tends to preoccupies the practitioners.

As it was stated earlier in Chapter One, in order to understand the reality of transfer the subject should not necessarily be approached by asking questions such as whether a particular purely role-related aspect of the learning takes place or not, rather the whole situation should be viewed from a wider perspective including the consequences of the training activity which are observable in the workplace.

When the subject of the learning was considered, it was purported that, by and large, the success of a training programme is determined not necessarily by the ability of the individual to perform the task alone but also by the factors present in the social context of the workplace which may or may not allow the occurance of the intended behaviour.

In the following discussions it will become evident to the reader that when a particular method is being considered for the successful realisation of positive transfer of the task-related aspects of a job, the social learning processes which are implicit within the use of such a method should also be given credit.

In order to highlight the importance of the social learning processes and their impact on the degree of effective transfer of a training programme, first the rationale behind the belief that some methods more than others result in improved transfer will be briefly considered. Then, in light of the above, the potential of each method will be considered in the context of whether or not and to what extent, a chosen training method may facilitate the integration of the learners (trainees) into the actual workplace.

Close to or away from the job

A closer examination of the literature on training and personnel development reveals that despite the presence of seemingly different views concerning the types of training methods, the writers concerned basically agree on [share a limited] a few criteria concerning their use. The major criteria used are;
- Where the training activity ought to be held?
- What is the nature of the training programme ?
- Who the programme is designed for ? and,
- What is the degree of the complexity of tasks to be
  learnt.

The above constitute the most popular criteria used for the classification of the training methods which are available to trainers. Glueck (1974) recommends that when considering training for unskilled or for obsolete employees, 'one of the four approaches which combine the elements of 'where' and 'what' of training' (p.330), must be considered. The four major methods recommended are in fact a variation of either on-the-job or off-the-job training methods. Beach (1980) like many other writers claims that major training modes are; on-the-job, vestibule and classroom training. In this way, lectures, conferences, role play and case studies have also been considered as methods and techniques which may be used to initiate and/or facilitate learning as variations of classroom training.

The most useful classification belongs to Miner (1969) and McGhee and Thayer (1961). They have used the proximity of the training locations to the actual workplace as the major criterion and suggest that there are two basic categories of training methods; on-the-job and off-the-job training. All other methods and techniques are seen as intermediate between these two extremes.

> Essentially we have a continuum, on one end is the on-the-job and on the other is the off-the-job training. Intermediate between these two extremes are the training methods called vestibule, apprenticeship and similar methods (McGhee and Thayer, 1961, p.180).

Major considerations

While McGhee and Thayer's rationale for classifying training methods into on and off-the job is a superior one, other contributing factors for choosing either of the above modes also need to be considered. For example, the off-the-job method is thought to be more suitable for learning tasks which are of a complex nature and therefore may require prolonged and uninterrupted periods of time spent on their learning.

The physical circumstances in the actual workplace may not provide the ideal situation for learning complex and difficult tasks, thus the training method which takes the individual away from the work environment is preferred. This is often the case where new technology, machinery and equipment are introduced and the present work force will require short training courses to either learn or update their knowledge and skills. In some cases the training is carried out by the suppliers of the technology rather than the receiving enterprise. For example, a firm of computer manufacturers takes on the responsibility of providing the relevant training as a part of an incentive package to further induce investment in the technology per se.

Generally, within industry in situations where the expertise for training staff is not available within the organisation, the task of ensuring that the relevant material is learnt and complex and difficult skills are acquired is left to outside agencies. The simpler the nature of the task, the more likely it is that some form of 'coaching' or 'sitting with Nelly' will be employed as an alternative.

Cost

It is generally true that cost is a determining factor as to whether the training should be carried out within the workplace or outside of it at a training centre (Kearsley 1982). The decision to send the employees to a training centre is often based on the anticipated and not necessarily the actual outcome. Cases have been reported where a group of skilled employees have been sent to an external training centre with the expectation that on their return they would be able to in turn impart the new knowledge and skills acquired to their fellow staff and workers, only to discover that the anticipated outcome has not materialised.

The unavailability of a training division within an organisation often results in the acceptance of more costly options and the use of an already set up training programme for upgrading or introducing new knowledge and skills. Often the potential cost in terms of damage to the new equipment and the likelihood of accidents, no matter how small, occurring while learning new skills on-the-job forces the employers to choose off-the-job methods as the least desirable but more practical option (Casio, 1982).

Altogether, some form of cost benefit analysis is desirable before deciding on the design of and alternative methods for implementing the training programme. With operatives and supervisory training programmes the traditional cost benefit analysis exercise can usually be easily carried out, mainly because the change in performance of the trainees in terms of improved productivity is normally measurable.

Woodward (1975), has shown that in cases of supervisory training, by calculating the benefits which the training programme is expected to yield against the cost involved, the ratio of benefit can be obtained. Should the cost and benefit ratio for training a group of employees be the same when considering the on or off-the-job options, the preference should be given to the method closer to the organisation which will also facilitate positive transfer.

When designing a training programme or simply choosing from amongst the options available, the nature of the job also needs to be considered carefully. This is different from the consideration which needs to be given to the complexities inherent in the job. For example, learning to work with computer controlled equipment may be considered to constitute a complex exercise, therefore off-the-job training may be called for.

When discussing the nature of a job there are a host of other issues such as whether or not the purpose of training is to initiate new knowledge, understanding, skills, attitudes or values, which have to be considered. Turner (1969) places these related issues in an ascending hierarchy with gaining knowledge classified as the least difficult and changing behaviour and attitudes as the hardest objective to achieve.

Observation has shown that lower categories of learnings such as increasing the knowledge and awareness of the employees about a new procedure, a production method or a new managerial policy can be safely attempted on an in-house basis. Skills too, depending on the degree of complexity, the availability of expertise and time needed for learning, and the suitability of the environment can be acquired on-the-job. Whereas, changes in attitude and values are often seen as the most difficult training activity and which often merit the use of specialised training centres.

In the latter situation, it has been observed that the chief reason for choosing the off-the-job training option has been based on the consideration given to the criterion of the 'availability' of resources within the organisation. What is often overlooked [not realised] is that the acquired changed attitudes and behaviours of the employees have to be informally approved by their colleagues, peers and superiors at work.

In the field of management training, in particular, the support of top management for realising positive transfer is crucial to the success of the training programme (Kakabadse, 1987).

Operative vs management training

Related to the above is the issue of whether or not the training programme is to be designed for and used to meet the training requirements of the operative or that of the management. More so, whether or not both the above categories of employees would benefit equally from an on-the-job training. First, a distinction which needs to be made is that the nature of the managerial job is inherently different from that of the operative. Managers are often held responsible for planning, organising and directing functions which are of a cooperative and strategic nature (Turner, 1969), whereas the operatives and shop floor employees task is often of an easily definable and measurable nature. In most cases, the employees' performance can be calculated and therefore the assumption is that training is usually used to realise or establish predetermined changes in behaviour or performance (Bramley, 1990).

Training in these cases involves the learning of a set of correct procedures. The aim of the training is to eradicate faults and to replace them with the approved (desired) methods of working. It is 'relatively easy to determine whether or not this has occurred: can or can not the operative work at the acceptable level?' (Warr et al 1971, p.22). Moreover, the fact that the jobs which are of a repetitive nature are usually carried out by unskilled and semi-skilled employees means that once a skill is acquired the daily repetition would facilitate the internalisation of the learnt material and thus accelerate the rate of positive transfer.

The managerial job, on the other hand, does not easily render itself to precise analysis. In addition to that in the hierarchy of skills, managerial training is rated as the most difficult one since it involves changes in behaviour, attitude and values, which are troublesome to analyse, define and evaluate once the training is completed. There are no 'correct' ways of managing organisations, 'with [management training] it is left to each individual trainee to attempt some integration of what has been learnt, to decide what aspects of it are relevant to his own job, and then to apply it as he thinks fit' (Warr et al, 1971, p.22).

The distinct differences between the nature of the task of the operatives and managers' job do not necessarily mean that all management training programmes should be carried out in centres outside of the organisation, but generally there has been a tendency to use off-the-job facilities for training managerial staff (Campbell, 1970).

Regrettably, in many cases it has been observed that the transfer of off-the-job management training, especially that which has involved the participation of management trainees from different cultures other than the one in which the training centre is located, is fraught with problems. In most of the above cases the consideration of 'fad' and 'fashion' has been the underlying influencing factor where the decision concerning the location of the management training has been concerned.

Operative training has traditionally used on-the-job methods, whereas in the field of management training and development, especially since the

1960's, it has been increasingly observed that off-the-job courses which are offered by an assortment of business and management centres are perceived by some employers to be the solution to the ineffectiveness of individual managers and the remedy for the inefficiency of the organisation as a whole.

The major issues, therefore, which are usually considered prior to opting for the on-the-job or off-the-job type of training are;
- The availability of in-house trainers and facilities.
- The extent of the complexity of the skills to be acquired.
- The comparative cost between the use of in-house or outside organisational training.
- The nature of the material to be learnt; knowledge, understanding, skills, attitudes and values; and,
- The type of training required whether operative or management.

Potential for effective transfer

As shown above, the issue as to whether or not a training method will result in better transfer to the actual job has not traditionally been given prime consideration. Observations made in industry revealed that training methods, depending on whether or not they are meant to integrate the trainees into the organisation, possess an inherent quality which contributes to the acceleration of the process of transfer.

Despite the apparent differences between the type of job, i.e. operative or managerial, the assumption that there is a direct relationship between the occurrence of positive transfer and the proximity of the learning situation to the actual workplace seems to remain a valid one.

To continue, in accordance with McGhee and Thayer (1961), two major categories, namely on-the-job and off-the-job will be used here for the analysis of the potential of the operative and management training for positive transfer. For the sake of simplicity supervisory training is also included in the operative category.

It is contended that the proximity of the learning situation and the trainee to the actual work environment provides the opportunity for social learning on his part and thus the potential for effective transfer is likely to be increased as the location of the training programme comes closer to the actual workplace. (See Figure 3.1)

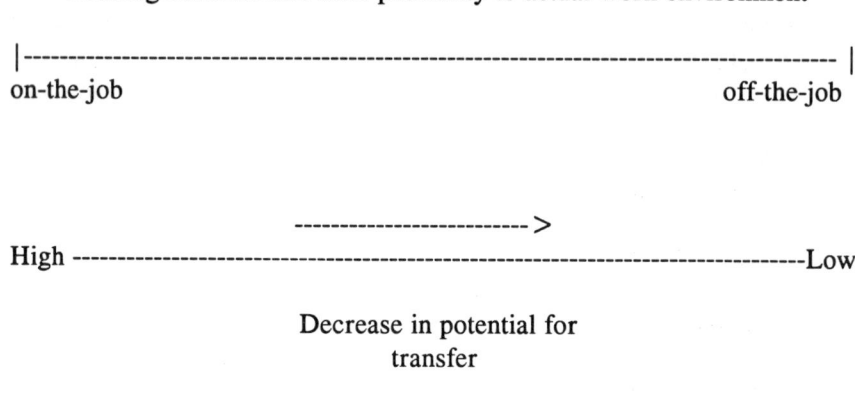

Training methods and their proximity to actual work environment

|--- |
on-the-job   off-the-job

                        ------------------------->
High --Low

                        Decrease in potential for
                                transfer

Within actual   Away from actual
  workplace   workplace

Figure 3.1   Continuum of the potential of on-the-job and off-the-job
             training modes, in relation to the proximity to the workplace
             social system

On-the-job training

Probably the most widely used method of training for shop floor
employees, formal and informal, is that of on-the-job (Gleuck, 1971). The
trainee is in both the physical and social environment of the workplace
thus simultaneously engaged in the process of acquiring both the technical
and social requirements of the job. However, the majority of writers on
the subject of training tend to place disproportionate emphasis on the
acquisition of the role-related requirements of the job rather than the social
ones. This is largely due to the subtle nature of the socialisation process
which the individual undergoes when fully or partially immersed in the
daily activities of the social system of the work organisation. Katz and
Kahn (1966) describe this kind of learning as responding to the
expectations of the role senders (peers, subordinates and bosses) which
specify the ways in which a job should be performed.
   Training on-the-job, which is commonly referred to within industry as
'sitting with Nelly', is a popular method. Most managers show a
preference for this mode of training unskilled and semi-skilled employees

because the trainee requires little special attention in terms of extra equipment or manpower and it usually results in some form of production. It is based on the policy of 'work while you learn'.

On-the-job training has advantages from the learning point of view, and is consistent with several principles of learning.

As the learning programme progresses, each successful attempt at doing the job will provide the trainee involved with the basis for reinforcement of the next learning stage. As Kenney and Reid (1986) argue, 'This is beneficial if he [trainee] is practicing correct method, but if not, he may be reinforcing errors which may be difficult to eradicate. It is, therefore, not entirely true that 'practice makes perfect' (p.132).

The availability of feedback from the experienced employee (old hand) provides the trainee with ample opportunities to gradually modify his performance to that which is recognised as effective by his colleagues and peers. As Miner (1969) states, 'active participation, and the more meaningful nature of the materials to the trainee, tends to minimise the problem of transfer to almost non-existence' (p.216). The trainee gradually becomes integrated into the workplace community which allows others to have the opportunity to become familiarised with the unique individual attributes, habits and 'ways of doing things' of the trainee concerned.

Despite the potentially high degree of effectiveness of this training mode, if it is not handled properly the ultimate cost can be high in damaged machinery, inferior products, dissatisfied customers (especially in the service industry), misfiled forms and badly taught and developed trainees (Gleuck, 1974).

Further, as indicated earlier, with the increasing rate of complexity of the technical content of training, this mode of training tends to become inefficient in so far as transfer is concerned. The reason being that in these cases, on-the-job learning must take second place to the primary function of the workplace; production, service or both (Stammer and Patrick, 1975). An example of this difficulty was observed in an organisation where the change over from a manually operated switch board to an electronically monitored system, led to low performance and a considerable lack of confidence and motivation on the part of the trainee operatives.

None-the-less, if on-the-job training programmes are properly utilised they can be of great value to industry. One of the most attractive features of this approach to training is that it provides the individual trainee with the opportunity to become familiarised with the norms, values and generally the dominant cultural value system of the work organisation

(Handy, 1985), while at the same time going through a process of acquiring the task-related knowledge, skills and values of the job.

However, it must also be considered that being present in the actual physical setting of the work organisation does not automatically lead to successful socialisation on the part of the trainee. Indeed, it is important for the trainee to come into contact with a variety of different work groups and be presented with the opportunity to spend some time with them in order to gain an overall understanding of the organisational culture.

The learning of the social processes which are inherent in this kind of training appears to take place more effectively where the technical demands of the job to be carried out, whether at manual or supervisory levels, are low in complexity. In this way, learning can be completed in a relatively short time. Support from colleagues, peers and especially superiors can accelerate the process of technical and social learning.

Becoming an apprentice

Apprentice training offers an integration of on and off-the-job learning which under ideal conditions is extremely effective. This approach is usually employed in order to prepare the trainee for a variety of skills and occupations (mostly of a non-managerial nature). For example, bakery, jewelry, engineering, diamond cutting, painting, ceramic cutting and tool making.

The apprentice system of training has been in use for a long time. Beach (1980) regards this method as 'a descendant of the craft guild system of the middle ages' (p.375). The apprentice normally commits himself to a period of intense training that involves both formal classroom learning and practical on-the-job experience during the training period. The prescribed period for completion of the technical nature of the job content may vary from two to as much as ten years (Glueck, 1974).

The position of 'apprentice training' on the proposed continuum of training methods and their potential for transfer (see Fig 3.1) is closer to the on-the-job extreme position than pure off-the-job training. In fact, because of the apprentice's link with the actual job situation, the apprentice method tends to be more successful in preparing the apprentice to perform effectively. The negative transfer of the learnt material from outside of to the workplace, tends to be minimised. This is due to long term supervision, motivation and the facilitating factors namely social learning processes to which the trainee is exposed in the actual workplace.

On the negative side, the presence of a well established hierarchy of skilled employees, with their accumulated years of experience and seniority, and a well recognised web of normative rules which almost everyone is expected to comply with, may inhibit those individuals, who could potentially benefit from creative and lateral thinking, from initiating new ways of performing the same task. Because, the standard for the performance and behaviour of the employee is well established, deviants are likely to experience an uncomfortable training period.

The prolonged nature of the apprenticeship also requires the trainee to show sustained commitment to the nature of the job. Continuous contact with the physical and social aspects of the workplace seems to ensure the apprentice's membership of its informal social system. This prolonged involvement with the society and culture of the workplace also assists the apprentice to enhance his knowledge and skills by incorporating the socially established and accepted body of knowledge present in the workplace, learning the tricks of the trade, into his formal training.

The government initiative during the last decade to provide incentives for industrial organisations to take on school leavers for a period of up to two years, on training schemes such as YTS (Youth Training Schemes) has been partly based an similar principles. Once the young trainee, in this case a school leaver, becomes accepted by the social hierarchy of the organisation his chances of becoming accepted by the organisation and later becoming a fully fledged employee are increased. The main drawback, however, is the perceived low status which is often associated with this sort of on-the-job training. The apprentice tends not to be fully guaranteed future employment.

In terms of its potential for positive transfer, it could be argued that, 'careful planning for transfer and precise determination of the learning content in integrated training should do more to render this method an effective training approach' (McGhee and Thayer, 1961, p.190).

Off-the-job training

Off-the-job training is a term which is used to describe any method other than those which involve the individual trainee in the actual workplace and which include simulation training and an assortment of training activities which are usually carried out in a classroom, vocational school, special learning centres and the like.

This mode of training includes a variety of diverse activities like lectures, seminars, conferences, case studies, demonstrations, simulations and games. Normally, this method is used by organisations with specific and complex training needs. It is not just a coincidence that large organisations are those which usually fit such descriptions and are reported to use this mode of training more frequently (Stromberg and Hill, 1964).

As was pointed out earlier in circumstances where, for example, the content of the job to be learnt is too complex; no qualified trainer or instructor is available; the learning requires the acquisition of higher order skills, attitudes and values; and the day to day pressures of the production inhibits effective learning, the use of training methods away from the actual workplace is regarded as a desirable and justifiable option.

Management training or retraining is usually carried out in specialised learning centres. The decision to choose off-the-job training instead of in-house ones is often based on the rationale that management training is about acquiring new values and attitudes and that they need to be acquired in specialised learning situations. It is in such centres that managers are expected to be transformed into active 'change agents' who once back in their organisations will promote the newly acquired values and beliefs and thus gradually change the old work culture to that which is more conducive to the achievement of planned goals (Ottoway, 1980).

The rationale that new values and attitudes need to be acquired away from the workplace, whilst it is appealing, has been rigourously questioned. This has led to considerable criticism of the use of off-the-job methods for management training. For example, it is conceivable that in order to achieve the above changes of attitudes in trainees, training instructors - apart from imparting technical knowledge - may attempt to instil social beliefs, attitudes and behaviours which differ from those present in the workplace (Analoui, 1990). However, on re-entry to the workplace the retrained individual is confronted with the existence of a well established social and cultural system and his newly imported values, attitudes and behaviours may not be compatible with those of the organisation.

> Learning undertaken in a specialised environment however does not necessarily transfer to reality and the very absence of some of the 'adverse' factors may mean that the trainee is not learning to cope with the actual situation (Kenney and Reid, 1986, p.141).

Thus, in order to regain and re-establish former work relationships, the individual trainee may have to re-adjust his behaviour in order to 'fit in' with his colleagues and superiors expectations. The individual trainee will therefore have to go through a process of corrective socialisation - often of an unofficial and discreet nature - which results in the delay of transfer. If, however, the individual fails to successfully complete this workplace social learning programme the expected 'lateral transfer' is inevitably doomed to be negative.

In order to avoid the negative aspects of using off-the-job methods, trainers attempt to 'build in' some form of 'reality' into the content and design of the training programme. The use of simulators has probably been one of the major steps in overcoming some of the transfer related problems which are usually associated with the use of training modes away from the 'real' workplace.

Simulation

This mode of training ensures that, during the course of training, the trainee learns to perform a task in an environment which simulates the real working situation (Glueck, 1974). When training concerns learning highly technical or complex task-related activities, it is suggested that 'The [training] centre provides an ideal environment simply because the disruptive and distracting element (i.e. excessive noise, stress etc) present in the actual workplace are greatly minimised' (Miner, 1969, p.214)

The use of simulators in aviation is becoming increasingly popular. With the aid of sophisticated computerised equipment pilots to be nowadays can be trained in an artificial environment which closely resembles the cockpit of the aircraft. The combination of vision, sound and changes in direction and movement which are created by corresponding movements of the hydraulic equipment beneath the simulator, provides the 'near reality' situation for trainees to learn, for example, how to take off or how to land the aircraft under specific weather conditions. In this way, should things go wrong during the training, extensive damage to an aircraft and injury or even death to passengers has been avoided.

Recent developments in the making of simulators has enabled the trainees to monitor and review their own performance while attempting, for example, a particular manoeuvre and they are now able to receive instant feedback on their progress. The use of video equipment in skilled and semi-skilled operatives training also results in the kind of feedback which is meaningful to the learner involved. The individual is placed in the position of observer of his own performance while learning a specific task. The use of the negative 'feedback loop' provides the trainee with indicators for adopting corrective measures when mistakes are made and ultimately will direct the trainee towards achieving the desired learning objectives.

The use of simulators to accelerate learning processes is no longer limited to the aviation industry. Nowadays, similar equipment is being used by 'schools' of motoring, the railways and also within the nuclear industry to teach trainees skills of a complex or delicate nature.

However, despite the apparent advantages, this form of off-the-job training does not constitute an economical option. In fact, unless large numbers of trainees, on a regular basis, use these purpose built centres which are equipped with simulators, the cost of running the simulated workplace will be more than that of financing the training in the actual workplace.

This is particularly so in the case of industries where the rapid changes in technology will inevitably result in the simulators becoming obsolete. For the management of such organisations the need to re-design or even purchase new simulators becomes a necessity, but not necessarily a value added alternative. 'For instance, flight simulators which allow the practice of a wide range of emergency procedures, cost airlines £50 million' (Bramley, 1990, p.40). It is, however argued that the benefits derived from the use of, for example, flight simulators for training pilots would outrun the cost of replacing a Tornado Jet.

Moreover, as the complexity of the task to be learnt increases, the use of workplace simulation training becomes more popular and wide spread in industry. It is believed that in principle the use of simulation will increase the effectiveness of the learning. In practice, however, it may result in a contraction of actual training effectiveness because of the poor transfer which is associated with training situations which are located away from the actual work environment.

It has also been suggested that despite the presence of similarities between the simulator and the actual equipment in the real work environment, the trainees can not escape the thought that the simulator 'is not the real thing'. The way in which an individual trainee subjectively perceives the simulator in use, affects his acceptance of the reality of the training situation in hand. It is the comparison between this perceived reality and the actual workplace situation which largely determines the success of the learning activity. If the simulator is not taken seriously by the trainees, on arrival in the actual workplace it may have a negative effect on whether or not the learnt skills are effectively recalled (transferred).

A major drawback associated with utilising simulators as training aids is that while training is in progress, the trainee is only exposed to the social value structure of a small primary training group which is temporarily created by the participants involved in the training location. The group values, attitudes to work and developed norms for acceptable standards of performance which are acquired during the training at the centre may not be compatible with those which prevail in the actual work environment. Thus, the trainee may experience disappointment and discouragement when he attempts to establish effective work relationships with his colleagues in the workplace on the basis of what he has learnt through the processes of socialisation at the training centre.

Often the off-the-job type of training is followed by an initial 'hands on experience' training period which provides the trainee with the opportunity to learn the necessary work related dominant social values and norms in order to successfully adjust to the new set of expectations, values and beliefs he finds himself confronted with. The greater the differences between the simulated social and technical environment and those of the actual workplace, the more likely that effective transfer will be delayed. The initial delay in the realisation of the transfer of learning from the learning environment to the job will compound the negative effects of low self-esteem and will lead to increased disappointment and discouragement on the part of the trainee.

Management training methods and transfer

Like their subordinates managers too require training and the opportunity to update their knowledge and skills. In their case, however, it is even more difficult to determine the exact amount of learnt material and how well the acquired skills and knowledge have been transferred. There are two major problems in devising a comprehensive scheme for the classification of the management training and development methods currently in use.

First, there is as much variety in the nature of the managerial jobs in industry as there are in the roles which managers play when doing their job (Copeman, 1951; Stewart, 1967; Mant, 1969; and Mintzberg, 1973). The second difficulty is one which is inherent in the hierarchy used to describe different managerial jobs (Melrose-Woodman, 1978). The managerial job can encompass anything from being a supervisor to a line manager and a top executive to a director who functions at board level. The differences in positions naturally imply differences in the nature of the jobs and thus the training needs of those concerned.

As a rule, it is possible to make the tentative generalisation that, as the managerial job ascends towards the upper levels of the hierarchy of the organisation, the individual trainees' need for technical techniques and manual skills diminishes considerably. A recent study of the management development and training needs of managers in the public sector (Analoui, 1991) reveals that altogether the task-related aspects of the managers job loses its importance for the position holder as he climbs the promotional ladder towards the positions at the strategic apex of the organisation. Intriguingly, however, the perceived need for the possession of skills and knowledge for controlling the social processes which dominate the activities of the people-related aspects of the workplace gains greater importance.

Using the framework offered earlier, based on the proximity of the training situation to the workplace, for classifying management training methods, it soon becomes apparent that despite the above mentioned differences, most of the available approaches in use for the training and development of managers fall into two main categories; either 'inhouse' on-the-job types or 'outside' off-the-job.

While 'inhouse' training encourages learning on the job through observation, experience and practice as well as trial and error, questioning and self correcting methods, the off-the-job (outside) methods rely heavily on the use of experts and specialised training centres. The framework which was developed earlier and used for analysing the potential of the methods to be used for 'operative' training can also be used to differentiate between the various approaches available for training 'managers'. For example, coaching and the use of inhouse methods can be equated to 'sitting with Nelly'. A type of training used to familiarise the semi-skilled and skilled employees with the skills and knowledge necessary to perform the task. At the other extreme position on the continuum of training methods and their proximity to actual workplace (see Figure 3.2), there are methods and techniques frequently used for training managers such as 'case study' and 'role play' which are very similar in principle to those of off-the-job types of training used for blue-collar employees. For example, in a role play training exercise the trainee managers are assigned a specific role from an actual or hypothetical case and are told to treat their role as close to reality as possible (Maier 1957). These sort of practices are very similar to 'simulation' equipment used for training the non-managerial staff. In either situations the proximity of the training centre to the actual workplace where the manager normally works constitutes the main criteria

70

for choosing a specific mode for training.

Inhouse   Outside

Within the   Away from the
actual   actual
workplace   workplace

High   --------------------------------->   Low
                  Potential for transfer

Continuum of the potential of the 'inhouse' and 'outside' management training and development modes for positive transfer in relation to the proximity to the actual workplace

Figure 3.2   Major category for management training and development
             methods

   As the proximity of the training situation to the actual workplace increases so is the potential for positive transfer of the trainee's learnt knowledge and skills to the job situation. Management training methods too indicate the presence of similar, if not identical, principals in so far as training of managers is concerned. Practitioners and training experts tell us that not only is it difficult to evaluate management training programmes (Turner, 1969; Glueck, 1974, Kakabadse and Mukhi, 1984), it is even more difficult to acknowledge that significant changes which should imply positive transfer within the workplace have occurred. In many cases the transfer is measured in terms of an overall increase in the effectiveness of the organisation as a whole (Nadler et al, 1979).

71

'Inhouse' management training methods

The on-the-job type methods which are usually used for the training and development of managers fall into the following three categories;
- Methods which require the trainee to closely work with someone who is already experienced in the job. The trainee is thus coached by that individual or group.
- Methods which place the trainee in someone else's position to do his job. Thus, expanding his knowledge and skills through doing a different job.
- Methods which place the trainee in charge of his own development with a greater degree of control, planning, design, choice of content of the programme and monitoring of his own progress.

Working with someone

Working with an experienced member of the organisation in order to learn from them or 'learning from experience' as it is traditionally referred to, constitutes a common approach to the training of managers, especially in the hotel and catering and service industries. Typically, a suitable individual is recruited and is instructed to work closely with an experienced manager, who enjoys an equal or relatively higher organisational status, in order to learn from him. The trainee is then coached by his colleague throughout the duration of training and his questions and queries are answered by the individual who has been made responsible for his development. Glueck (1974), contends that 'one of the best methods of developing a new managers is for effective managers to teach them. The coach superior sets a good example of how to be a manager' (p.371). The effective manager in this case takes the new comer under his 'wing' and 'teaches him the ropes'.

As far as the learning of the task-related aspects of the job are concerned, the progress of the individual is largely determined by how enthusiastic he is about his prospective job, the effectiveness of the inhouse instructor and, by and large, the ability and experience of the coach to create a climate conducive to learning (Mace, 1958).

The support provided by the coach is probably the single most important factor in the occurrence of effective transfer. The process of entry or re-entry into the organisation, after a long period of training, is naturally fraught with uncertainty and anxiety for the individual concerned. Continuous support from the coaching staff minimises the harmful effects of the 'transition process' for the trainee. (Adams et al, 1976).

Working closely with others, being coached and guided relentlessly on almost every issue or activity at work could place the trainee in a 'tight spot' whereby he is not given personal space to, for example, make decisions or even make mistakes if necessary, to learn from them. Probably the most valid criticism of all is that although the trainee gradually earns the recognition and respect of his colleagues and obtains his membership to the informal social system of the work community, the drawback is that he may solely adopt the prevailing philosophy and management practices (Argyris, 1964).

The on-the-job nature of the training provides the trainee with an opportunity to learn the social aspects of working with his peers, subordinates, superiors and even the clients of the organisation, thus facilitating the process of speedy transfer.

From time to time, situations do arise where a manager who has a 'flair' for working with others - competent with social and interactive skills - and can 'get on with' others, becomes over institutionalised to the extent that he will refrain from initiating change in the workplace even though he sees it is necessary. The reason for this, in most cases, is the unwillingness on the part of the newcomer to 'rock the boat' and thus become ostracised by his colleagues and peers at work.

Conversely, many situations have been observed where an individual trainee manager who has benefited from excellent task-related knowledge and skills has been rejected by the membership of the social system of the organisation and labelled as an ineffective employee solely on the ground that he had not been able to get on with others. Regular coaching and the provision of counselling opportunities, although a costly and time consuming activity, can offer an effective supplementary means of overcoming some of the negative aspects associated with on-the-job management training methods.

In someone else's shoes

Placing an individual in a post other than his own, whether on a temporary or a semi-permanent basis is typically referred to as 'job rotation'. Job rotation or 'sitting in place of Nelly' is used as a managerial strategy in order to motivate managers and employees and simultaneously broaden their knowledge and skills. In small organisations, especially in situations where there are similarities between the jobs, the use of this method for training is recommended. Problems, however, may arise in a

73

situation where the job rotation exercise involves physical and geographical transfer. In such situations the individual manager involved is expected not only to learn the task-related aspects of the new job but also is implicitly expected to successfully undergo the socialisation training courses in his path. Many managers see the request to transfer as a manipulative strategy on the part of their superiors which is exercised by the organisation to prohibit the individual from 'growing roots' in one department, branch or district. Certainly a systematic approach to job rotation, as a means for initiating serious training, should involve some degree of coaching and counselling both during and after the training is over.

In the hotel and catering industry in particular, it has been observed that frequent and unplanned transfers which do not allow for the learning processes to be completed in one place before being moved to next, often results in the alienation of the managers concerned and it may even lead to the resignation of staff and a high management turnover.

Where managers of departments or establishments who were in job rotation schemes were allowed to remain in one place long enough to learn what was required, they naturally initiated changes to the work culture i.e. the way things were done in that work setting, which were not necessarily compatible with either their predecessors or successors' ways of doing things. As a result the employees of these organisations frequently found themselves confronted with different expectations from their bosses. The high rate of staff turnover and inefficiency experienced in these organisations can directly be attributed to the unintended consequences of such adhoc intervention schemes.

Be responsible - do it yourself

This approach to management training is not necessarily purely an inhouse training programme. It may involve 'outside' training such as attending short courses, seminars, conferences and such like. The attractive feature of this approach to training and development is the meaningfulness of the learning activities for the individual trainees concerned and the presence of commitment on their part to completing a self improvement programme.

In many organisations the resources available are not adequate to satisfy the training needs and demands of the individuals, thus, the need for incorporating both types of training is necessary and justifiable. For example, an individual who is primarily placed in charge of the identification of his own training needs, the design, implementation and

74

However, this temporary social system lacks the day to day reality of the actual workplace and requires the management trainees to become involved in the kind of informal learning processes which may or may not form a useful part of their armoury of acquired managerial knowledge and skills, once they are physically transferred back to the real world of work.

Serious trainers are aware of the fact that for the sake of maintaining 'harmony' and 'order' which is normally expected from a manager - at least in western societies - managers on a group training course generally avoid prolonged criticism of their colleagues with whom they may have to continue working after the training is completed. Managers are usually expected to be extrovert, team makers, to get on with others and generally to seek consensus and act as a group. This inevitably prohibits them from adopting, creative, individualistic and novel approaches to solving problem situations.

In real management situations, conflict is as much a part of the managers' work as is his cooperation and collaboration with others. Moreover, the outside training situation often lacks the presence of 'pressures and stressful situations' which are characteristics of this type of job. However, sometimes in order to learn the new values, attitudes and skills which are required to be able to deal with the task and people and for which there are no resources, provisions or experts within the organisation, 'outside' training methods, from time to time, have to be used.

In these situations consideration should be given to the relevance of the course content as well as the balance between the task-related aspects of training programmes and the social learning processes. Building 'reality' into outside types of management training methods and techniques may mean considering a combination of exposure to 'inhouse' and 'outside' programmes on a sequential basis. What remains a dilemma is that as the managerial training methods move away from the actual manager's job, the learning processes are intensified (especially learning the higher order values, attitudes and the like) but the transfer of the learnt material to the job is significantly reduced. Since the social system of the organisation with its inherent implicit social learning processes is the significant contributing factor in the case of 'inhouse' training and in the case of 'outside' training, in terms of its absence from training situation, it can safely be deduced that the proximity to the actual workplace environment during the training is an undeniable contributing factor to effective transfer.

Conclusion

Training methods, whether used for 'operative' or 'managers', on an on or off-the-job basis, tend to act as a vital bridge between the learning processes on one hand and their transfer to the actual workplace on the other. In the field of operative training the use of on-the-job techniques is more prevalent. This is partly due to the nature of the knowledge and skills required to improve the operative's performance and productivity. Management training and development, on the other hand, has often been implemented outside of the organisation, in the hope that the learning of behavioural skills, complex concepts, values and new attitudes will be facilitated.

Examination of the two main categories of training methods has revealed that, as the location of the training programme moves away from the actual workplace, the potential for more effective transfer is adversely affected, to the extent that in the case of some off-the-job training programmes this may even result in the occurrence of negative transfer. Conversely, as the location of training programmes (activities) is brought closer to the workplace, the individual trainee is provided with the opportunity to interact with his future work colleagues, subordinates, peers, bosses and clients, which in turn leads to an increase in the effective transfer of the learnt material.

Inherent in the use of any type of off-the-job training is the inevitability of being exposed to the informal, yet influential, primary training group social learning processes. This experience may have a negative effect when the transfer of learnt material is expected to occur positively on the job within the actual workplace.

When decisions on selecting the location and nature of training are being made, consideration also needs to be given to cultural background, workplace ethos and value systems. Such an analysis ought to form an indispensable part of considering an appropriate means by which the training objectives are to be realised.

Finally, a combination of on-the-job and off-the-job methods, for training operatives, and inhouse and outside training, for managers, could positively affect the process of initiating and accelerating the realisation of effective transfer of learning to the actual workplace.

4 Socialisation: An invisible learning programme

Introduction

The results of every training scheme, whether of an on or off-the-job nature, will eventually be taken to the actual workplace. This is where the transfer of learning is expected to take place, hopefully in a positive form. It is, however, of significant importance to remember that basically a training programme, regardless of where it is carried out, entails two main but interrelated aspects of learning.

The first aspect which is commonly over emphasised, encompasses the constituent planned and 'formal' learning processes. These intended learning activities have already been identified as being associated with the technical aspects of a training programme. A typical example of this kind of learning is where an employee's performance is viewed as not being 'up to date', thus he is sent to participate in a training programme which is specifically designed to elevate his performance from its present (unsatisfactory) level to a level which is regarded as desirable (satisfactory). That is, to fill the perceived task-related knowledge or skill gap of the employee concerned. The task-related aspects of learning are easily identifiable, particularly in cases where off-the-job types of training methods are to be used.

The second aspect of learning which is of an informal nature and is often not primarily planned for, takes place in the actual workplace. Here, this vital phase of learning has been identified as the social-related aspects of training. In the case of on-the-job training it occurs almost simultaneously with the task-related aspect of the training.

The social-related learning processes and the extent of their impact on the transfer of learning to the job situation have hitherto been largely neglected. Admittedly, it is difficult to plan for, execute or to systematically evaluate the possible outcome of these subtle and perspicacious learning activities

In almost all training schemes considerable emphasis is placed on the former learning processes thus, unintentionally, the significance of the social learning processes which are well camouflaged within the daily activities in the actual workplace, has been grossly undermined.

This inescapable informal learning programme, commonly referred to as 'socialisation', which in the case of newcomers and trainees is initially intensive, has to be completed by almost every one, from the gate keeper to the executive members of the organisation, before they become accepted as a 'full member' of the workplace social community. Most training programmes do not take into account these 'later learning' processes. In fact, in most cases it has been observed that the individual newcomer or trainee is left entirely to his own devices as far as becoming familiar with these pertinent, crucial and decisive learning activities is concerned. In these situations, in so far as transfer is concerned, learning by 'trial and error' seems to be the order of day.

In this chapter, first the importance of socialisation as a learning process to which all trainees will inevitably be subjected and its 'make or break' effect on the outcome of the training programme, will be discussed. Then, the transition model will be employed to explain the typical phases of social learning that an individual goes through and finally, the implications of the above in the case of four identified types of training situation will be discussed with specific reference to the degree of effective transfer of the already learnt task-related aspect of training to the actual job situation.

Socialisation at work: the neglected learning processes

Experienced managers and training specialists are aware of the presence of and influential nature of the socialisation processes at work. When a newcomer or a trainee joins the work organisation it is not uncommon to hear it said that he should be given the time and space to find his place or that it takes time to find 'a niche' for himself and to learn the ropes. Yet, surprisingly, almost all accounts provided in the available literature on transfer tend to completely overlook this set of informal learning processes. The most likely explanation for this neglect could be that these ever present learning activities are usually planned, initiated, implemented and regulated purely on an informal basis. Whereas the task-related learning processes, being a part of the formal system of the organisation, are usually operated and controlled visibly and openly and with the aid of established and recognised rules and procedures, regulations and policies of the organisation (Roethlisberger and Dickson, 1939).

It was in fact Mayo, an industrial psychologist and his colleagues, who discovered the presence of the social system which largely determines the degree of job satisfaction that the individual receives and for which the organisation does not necessarily plan.

Before embarking upon delineating how the informal or social-related learning can influence the realisation of the task- related aspects of a training programme, it is important to become familiar with the meaning of the term socialisation itself. The term socialisation is referred to as 'the process by which the individual learns to become a member of society (Nobbs, 1983, p.5).

Each organisation has its own unique social system which is comprised of the most important of its constituents - people, who actively influence as well as are influenced by the learning processes inherent within the social structure of the workplace. With the growing influence of the work of the Human Relations school, more emphasis was being placed on 'group' dynamics as opposed to the 'individual's' role within the organisation. Managers and practitioners began to plan for the task to be carried out in group form, thus increasing the motivation of the individuals towards achieving a higher standard of performance.

Unfortunately, many, including eminent writers in the field of organisation studies, began to think that individuals played a rather less significant role in the creation of the body of norms and the value system of the organisation. The informal system of the workplace, therefore, was primarily seen as being created and controlled by the contribution of the members of the 'primary' groups in the workplace (Watson, 1980). This, however, should not be seen as an underestimation of the extent of the influence of the informal social system on individual and group work behaviour.

The basic components of the informal system of any organisation are the individuals who perform at various levels of the hierarchy. As Kempner (1987) aptly asserts, 'The term informal organisation is no longer applied exclusively to social groups but refers to all relationships in the organisation that are not officially prescribed or expected' (p.182).

For the trainer it is imperative to recognise that as Brown (1965) suggests, the primary (informal) organisation of industry consists of five separate levels:

1. The total informal organisation [organisation is viewed as a system of interlocking groups of all types].

2. Large group, usually comprised of individuals sharing similar interests or having similar opinions regarding specific organisational or work-related issues. The members of unions or other related associations who are bound by accepting certain regulatory rules and norms which affects their job related performance are included in this category.

3. The primary 'clique' or work group who share a particular task and often share a specific job location. For example, a group of miners or a specific shift, firemen who work in one station and share a specific responsibility, nurses who work in the theatre and the executive members of the board are all examples of this kind of group.

4. Small groups, usually a part of the primary group in which two or more individuals mutually adjust their activities with one another and collectively co-ordinate their own activities. Small groups of this kind because of the cohesive nature of the social and technical relationship amongst its members, tend to develop their own sub-cultures which possess its own normative rules and regulations for carrying out work and conduct towards one another.

5.The individual who rarely participates in social activities within the organisation.

The trainee or newcomer to the organisation may become a member of one or a few social groups. While the total informal system is exerting influence on the behaviour and attitude of the individuals, it is usually the primary group which has a more determining effect towards changing the attitudes and behaviours of the people. Therefore, it now becomes apparent why, for example, when two individuals who have entered the same organisation at around the same time, at least from the point of view of the primary group socialisation, are likely to have experienced the process of induction differently.

We have all experienced the feeling of being 'socialised'. Socialisation takes place almost immediately and ruthlessly from the moment that the individual appears on the scene of the organisation. As Schien (1965), appropriately observes, 'organisations socialise their members by creating a series of events which serve the function of undoing the old values so the person will prepare to learn new values' (1965, p.110). The task of learning the new values is not just confined to becoming familiar to the ways in which people are expected to socially interact with one another, it also and equally applies to performing the task-related aspects of the job.

The informal social value system tends to regulate the ways in which tasks are to be performed. An individual, in our case a trainee, who has been taught to carry out a particular task in a certain way may discover that the prescribed way to do the job may not be approved of by the informal social norms and value system of the workplace, thus gradually he will feel that pressure is being placed on him to 'mend his ways'.

Hunt (1979) asserts that 'The behaviour change in the new member may be little more than that he or she is doing a job in a situation he or she was not in previously. But the change is likely to be more substantial than this. Attitudes, values, identification and friendships patterns are all likely to be affected by the move in to a new organisation' (p.160).

Of course, the intensity of the social learning processes experienced by the trainee - or the retrained employee - varies according to the degree of complexity of the social system, type of organisation, size, level and nature of the task to be performed and number of immediate (primary) groups with whom the individual ought to work and collaborate. To make matters worse, the learner (the newcomer) is also expected to perform a job and to carry out a task of some technical nature for which he is employed or specially trained. Above all he is expected to perform effectively and to 'pull his weight'.

The above process of 'doing' the job and 'learning' the social-related aspects of the job and the organisation as a whole, may not occur on a consecutive basis. It has frequently been observed that the individual is exposed to both aspects of learning simultaneously.

To 'make' or 'break'

Segelman (1973) deals with the 'socialisation' processes in the context of the organisation. He ascertains that the organisation shapes the values and definitions of newcomers. It provides meaning for interaction and events and guides them in what they must do if they are to 'make it'. In this context, to 'make it' refers to the outcome of going through the social learning processes and coming out in one piece. Other writers have also referred to the importance of managing the socialisation processes.

Some organisations tend to employ the well known policy of the 'sink or swim' (Kennoy and Reid, 1986); whereby the individuals (the newcomer or the trainee) involved, who are often new to the job, are left to fend for themselves. The adoption of such measures is less than desirable, if effective 'transfer' is expected to materialise.

To the unsuspecting trainee who has successfully survived the arduous performance-related learning processes, the worries and difficulties are seemingly over. The main learning tasks are apparently completed. The trainee sees himself as qualified and equipped with the necessary knowledge and skills to under take the new responsibility. What he is not warned about is the presence of social 'traps' and entanglements which can prove to be extremely trying, if not painful in nature, but which have to be negotiated.

It is not an exaggeration to suggest that within the social boundaries of the work organisation, a challenging social learning assault course is awaiting the newcomer. These social processes proffer continuous obstacles and the failure to negotiate them successfully, can have serious implications for the individual concerned. Since this informal training programme (socialisation) has been tested, used and evaluated over and over again by all the existing members of the organisation, the accumulation of up to date information within the consciousness of the system, the availability of resources and the plentifulness of advisers, instructors and evaluators, makes this social learning programme a perfect one.

Socialisation is basically a complicated package of learning processes in which the materials to be learnt are values, norms and beliefs, sometimes in shared and sometimes in unshared forms. Also there are informal rules and regulations, unwritten codes of conduct, custom and practices whose main function is to regulate the ways things are done in that organisation.

Socialisation, an on-the-job induction programme, is equally applied to the lower levels of occupational groups, to the middle management and to the executive levels. All newcomers to the society of the workplace will have to encounter social training 'instructors', ranging from the porter to the top executives, each employing the task in hand or the job for which they are trained as a means or channel for communication with others and even as a basis for reward and punishment or retribution.

Extensive personal association with various organisations in industry has revealed many cases where the trainee who has just completed a final training programme had to start again a further phase of informal learning, so as to become familiar with new values and systems, definitions and meanings which are conveyed to him or her, by subtle but effective means. A production manager in a medium sized engineering factory explained how he had to 'learn the hard way' when he completed his three months production management training course and returned to work.

> Having gone through the course, I could now see what were the major reasons for so much waste and inefficiency in the work shops. At first, it felt so good to see that all that hard work was going to pay off and I could actually put into use the new concepts and techniques which I had learnt. But little did I know, the moment I opened my mouth in the monthly meeting with a proposal to change the layout to create more room for storage and to put a stop to unnecessary practices, all hell broke loose on me. The proposal was accepted alright, but I could feel something was not right. When it came to actually implementing the new layout for the machines everything went wrong. There was more waste in that part of the workshop than the whole shopfloor, never mind the breakages and damage to the equipment. It was not just the shopfloor that was reluctant to accept the change, my colleagues too did not seem to be happy about it and kept criticising the new layout. At last we had to scrap the idea and all that was left was embarrassment for me.
>
> When I asked Gordon the senior production manager why, he said "The rumour is that it happens to guys who want to push new ideas all by themselves and not share the glory with their colleagues. Listen Bill, (he lowered his voice) we all know what needs to be done, but knowing is one thing and doing it is a different matter.. if you get my meaning".

Adomaitis (1984) in her study of slimming organisations, reports how the technical requirement for carrying out the task of 'group leader' was over emphasised and was assumed to constitute an essential aspect of the leadership training. Thus, potential recruits were subjected to an intensive off-the-job training whose content was basically of a technical nature and did not provide the 'leaders' with adequate socio-psychological skills to do their job effectively. Further, she successfully demonstrated how the performance of the members of the slimming group (in terms of reaching their target weights) was greatly determined by the complex process of social interactions which took place amongst them and in and outside of the club, rather than by the technical aspects of slimming which the group leader had been taught to focus attention on.

It is believed that the social learning processes, which are generally of an informal nature, in part constitute the necessary link for making the completion of effective transfer of learning to the job situation possible.

Regulating mechanism

The process of 'socialisation' acts as a powerful regulating mechanism. Its degree of influence on people's attitude and behaviour can be measured by the ways in which the task performance and social conduct and related activities of the newcomers to the organisation have been altered. For instance, a typist, a piece worker or even a junior executive who has undergone off-the-job training may soon discover that although the possesion of a high level of commitment or performance is recognised and even actively encouraged by their superior or training instructors, their improved or superior performance may infuriate their colleagues because the well established and rigourously obeyed social norms have been ignored.

The paradox becomes more apparent when a trainee, who has successfully completed an extensive course of training and has achieved the level of 'acceptability' which is expected from him by his instructors and organisational peers, has to consciously and voluntarily throw away the status of 'acceptability' in order to be accepted by his colleagues, thus gaining permission to become a part of the social system.

Social requirements at organisational level or in the actual workplace prove their dominance and self regulating nature over the purely technical or job related aspects of work (Analoui, 1990). In essence, people in the social context of the organisation begin to learn to react to and interact with each other and the situations within which they operate. 'People pick up cues and offer responses in return. The degree to which these responses are recognised as appropriate depends on the norms and values determining that situation' (Kakabadse, 1982, p.111).

However, if newcomers (including trainees) fail to pick up these subtle cues and directions provided by their colleagues and co-workers, a series of reprimanding responses will be directed towards them. These can range from overt hostility to social ostracism and even attempts of sabotage to their performance. For example, in a medium sized manufacturing company, the author observed how a manager who had just undergone the company induction training course failed to recognise the limits of his responsibilities. As a consequence the manager's commendable 'transferred' performance was viewed and labelled as "creeping to the MD". His improved performance was repeatedly sabotaged by his colleagues, so that he eventually 'came to see the light'. His superior described this experience as learning to 'know what the score was'.

This kind of experience is not an unusual phenomena; the bitter nature of confrontation with unidentified social pressures usually directs people towards undertaking a process of reconciliation with those realities. Similarly, for the individual apprentice or trainee who has been absent from the organisation for a long time, it is commonly necessary for him to renew his social membership and to acquire (or update) the social skills that are viewed as important by the reference individuals or groups within the social system of the work environment.

The socialisation process, as it will be dealt with in the next chapter, need not necessarily be regarded as having a negative effect on the smooth and effective transfer of the skills and knowledge to the actual job. Socialisation or the learning processes which it consists of can be identified and their acquisition can be facilitated in order to increase and improve the rate of social learning for the individual trainee concerned.

The significance of the importance of the above set of learning processes has, as yet, not been fully recognised and therefore the lessons learnt have not been fully incorporated in a systematic way into training programmes with the aim of improving transfer. While many practitioners and training specialists are aware of the reality and significance of socialisation, the role of induction training which is offered to new employees is often chiefly viewed as a means for familiarising them with the physical as well as the human aspect of the work environment.

It must be noted that it would be simplistic, if not naive, to equate the complex prolonged process of socialisation with the brief induction training. Induction training aims to familiarise the individual trainee or newcomer, with the formal rules, procedures and regulations governing the ways in which things are expected to happen. Sometimes, the trainers and instructors involved plan, include and impart the necessary working knowledge which represents some aspects of the 'real life' from the informal social system of the organisation to the trainees. But, induction training is a formal and systematically planned on-the-job learning activity which aims to institutionalise the individual employee, to teach them the correct and legitimised ways of doing the job. This formal training, of course, facilitates the socialisation, but does not take its place.

Socialisation, in essence, is an assumed task which is carried out 'naturally' and in an informal manner, though sometimes unconsciously.

The contributors are the individuals and group members who make up the community of the workplace, whether it be a primary group or the total informal system.

Some writers on organisation obviously are not clear about the main difference between the 'formal' and 'informal' nature of and the differences in the constituent ingredients of an induction training programme and the socialisation processes. The fact is that a properly planned induction phase of training can help the socialisation process along and assist the individuals involved to get over the initial shock and subsequent learning difficulties. As Hunt aptly remarks, 'The process of induction is designed to make the changes (or socialisation) as easy and as predictable as possible' (1979, p.160).

To summarise, while nowadays, it is widely accepted that socialisation is about the necessity to change, not many writers describe these changes or difficulties which new employees and trainees experience with social learning, let alone admit that these are specific social learning processes which are job related and are inherently different from those task-related and technical ones. Even fewer writers, especially those concerned with training, have acknowledged the direct relationship between the socialisation processes and the occurrence of positive transfer, nor have they attempted to satisfactorily explain this predominantly organisational phenomena in the context of technical and social learning. It is for this reason that, it is believed, training specialists and serious practitioners need to know how transition, which encompasses the three stages of learning associated with the socialisation process, operates in reality and how the trainees will act and react to each of these stages of learning in their attempt to negotiate the reality of transfer.

Transition and negotiation of social reality

It is unsatisfactory to tell trainees that the social learning processes which occur during the course of socialisation are of the utmost importance, but not to enable them to see how they occur and how they can be effectively coped with. Most trainers are familiar with the concept of change. After all training, whether it is carried out on-the-job or conducted outside of the physical boundaries of the workplace, is used as a means of initiating and realising a planned change of some sort.

Changes in people's performance, behaviours, attitudes and values are the results which are expected from a training programme. It, however, becomes rather disturbing to see that some trainers or practitioners see the completion of the formal course of learning as a guarantee of the occurrence of the desired change. The changed or altered behaviour and attitudes to work are then expected to be displayed at work in a most taken for granted fashion. Of course many such expectations are dashed.

It was noted earlier that a satisfactory explanation for the occurrence of transfer needs to also consider other changes which one has to go through once one enters the actual workplace. Whether the individual employee has just joined the organisation and his on-the-job training course has just begun or whether he has returned from an intensive course of off-the-job training, on his arrival he is in both cases expected to behave in a manner which is organisationally acceptable.

Basically, it is expected that members of an organisation will do things in a way which is agreeable to their colleagues and peers, bosses and even the clients of that particular organisation. This calls for a lot of new learning to be done and changes to become accustomed to before being accepted a as fully fledged member of that organisation. Socialisation is about this inevitable change process which has to be negotiated by the trainee.

Transition and socialisation

Transition as a concept provides a useful tool for understanding how individuals come to terms with the reality of change. Accordingly, transition is defined as 'movement from one area to another or change from one state to another' (Reber, 1985). While the concept of transition has been around since the beginning of 1960's and has been developed and used by psycho-therapists, counsellors and more recently management developers for explaining the adjustment to career change, it is not directly and specifically used for throwing light on the complex problem of transfer in the context of socialisation and its related learning processes.

Originally, the concept of transition was developed by researchers who were concerned with the effects of change on people and how, for example, patients with terminal diseases coped with the notion of dying and eventually faced death as a final learning experience.

The most important contribution was made by Haze and Hopson (1976) for mapping out the cycle of transition as stages for dealing with change of various kinds. The generalisation of the use of the concept for understanding the various changes which the individual does experience throughout the change cycle was later developed by Parker and Lewis

(1980) at the Cranfield School of Management. They successfully showed that the changes which an individual is about to experience do not necessarily have to be death or the loss of an important reference person before one qualifies as experiencing transition. Changes at a smaller scale, such as getting divorced and even promotion to a more senior position, though regarded as a positive event, still necessitates going through a period of transition. The most commonly used ground for the use of transition is for exploring the fluctuation of an individual recruit's performance when he or she joins the organisation.

The above writers most unique contribution to the development of the subject, is probably their exploration and identification of the different stages which are involved in transition and thus offering an insight into the management of the process as a whole. The original phases which were identified in a typical transitional case related to the typical experiences of an individual whilst negotiating the reality of change and the steps which had to be taken to cope with that change.

The first of these stages is the *immobilisation* which is experienced due to the initial shock. For example, making a 'bad' and/or unexpected discovery or hearing some exceptionally 'good' news. This stage will be closely followed by *denial*, a psychological state which is typically shown by the affected individual and which is characterised by behaviour which suggests that they are unable to accept the new reality with which they are faced. For example, the affected individual who has recently experienced a bereavement would insist that the death of a close relative had not taken place, or the car had not been stolen. Statements such as 'I could hardly believe what I read', explains the inner feelings of the individual in facing the early stages of transition. The third stage of the transition cycle is clinically known as *depression*. This is often manifested through displaying a lack of interest, enthusiasm and generally lacking the energy and concentration for carrying on with the daily activities or operations.

Psychologists tell us that self-pity, low self-esteem, feelings of dependency and a perceived lack of personal worth are typical responses to change at this stage of transition. At work a sharp decline in the performance and quality of one's work, a tendency to become inner-orientated and hence avoiding social gatherings and activities are observed to constitute common responses on the part of those who experience this stage of transition. Depression at its highest point, depending on the level of shock received by the individual involved, the magnitude of the change and his previous experiences of similar changes, personality type and other related factors, will be epitomised by a complete feeling of helplessness.

Kakabadse et al (1987) successfully illustrates how this stage of experiencing transition can alter the degree of work effectiveness displayed by the individual. It is also argued that the above stage constitutes the most crucial phase in coping with change.

If the transition process has been carried out effectively the individual will carry out the next stage which is *letting go* of the old values and accepting the new values whatever they may be. The individual begins to consider the 'now what?' scenario. For example, the transfer from one department to another, one region to another, a different cultural location, a job with different responsibilities and specifications from the previous one becomes the reality and the individual begins to accept it as it is. This stage which marks the early stages of recovery is marked by *testing the new reality*.

An individual who, for example, has experienced losing a partner will now attempt successful interaction with others who may fall into the category of 'potential partner'. At this stage the individual still suffers from ineffectiveness but recovery is in sight. Learning new values by deliberately discarding the old ones and actually accepting the new reality becomes the order of the day.

It is probably apparent to the reader with even a limited experience of dealing with people at work, that 'transition is for real', though unfortunately the individual who experiences the above chain of psychological states may not be aware of the process itself.

The transition cycle of the socialisation process

In order to understand how transition works and see its relevance for the transfer of learning to the job, a hypothetical case of a trainee who, after a long period of being away on a training course, returns to the workplace will be used here. The phases of social learning that the individual has to go through to complete the process before either becoming effective or remaining ineffective, with very little of his acquired knowledge and skills being transferred to his job, are indeed similar to those described earlier, when the process for coping with change was discussed.

There are, however, differences between the two processes. In the main, the trainee returning to the workplace, his experience of 'shock', 'denial', 'depression', 'discarding', 'testing' and ultimately and hopefully 'integration' may not be as noticeable, at least to the individual himself, as is the case, for example, with the person who experiences the sudden and

91

perhaps unexpected change involved in moving into a new job. Nevertheless, the effects of the transition on the performance of the trainee is noticeable, at least to the training specialists and learned managers with or for whom the trainee works.

Three distinct stages

There are three separate but interrelated phases in a transition process which the trainee is likely to go through while simultaneously learning to cope with the social reality of the workplace. These are, 'initiation', 'negotiation' and 'integration' (see Figure 4.1).

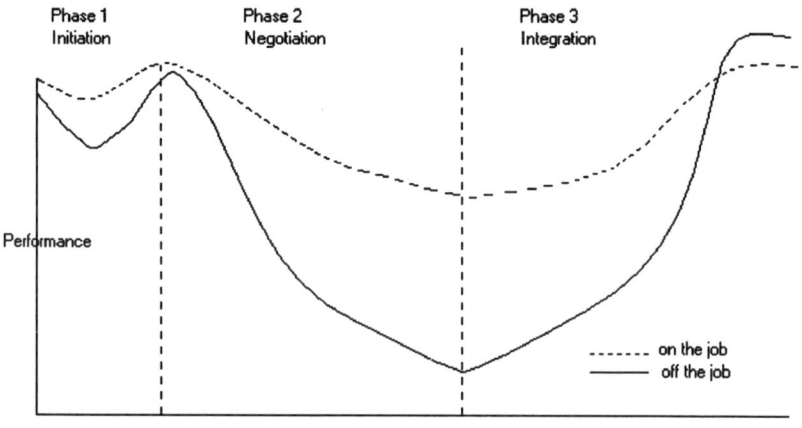

Time spent in the actual workplace

Figure 4.1   The phases in socialisation and transition of on-the-job and off-the-job situations

For the transfer of learning to be positively materialised, the individual needs to successfully complete the above socialisation phases. Thus becoming fully integrated into the social system of the organisation. Only then, providing the task-related aspect of the training had been successfully completed, and when the ethos of the primary group or the organisation, as a whole, is conducive for trying out newly learnt skills and knowledge,

92

can positive transfer be expected to be fully realised.

Initiation The individual trainee, at this stage of socialisation, is not likely to experience substantial learning of the social norms and values which govern the performance of the task and the general conduct of his peers or colleagues. The nature of the interactions with his peers and colleagues are typically frustrated by the elements of uncertainty and feelings of apprehension which stem from not knowing what changes have taken place in the individual trainee.

For new employees and ones returning from training centres outside the organisation, the 'tolerance' on the part of colleagues and peers is high and the individuals are given ample room and space to manoeuvre. They are basically 'left alone' to familiarise themselves with the 'place'. The newcomer or returner tend to manage the task-related aspects of the work mainly by using the previously learnt skills and expertise which had proven useful. Whether such task-related knowledge and skills are carried over by a trainee from the period prior to being sent off to the training centre, or that the individual who is being transferred from one post to another had learnt them in his previous position, hardly matters.

In fact, during this initial phase of socialisation a great deal of emphasis is placed on finding out whether or not the new recruit or the newly trained employee measure up to the routine and physical aspects of the job. For the trainee, the first day back in the office (manager) or behind the machinery (operative) will seem much longer and the job (even if returning to the same one) will seem to be more strenuous, tiring and harder to manage.

Soon the trainees will become accustomed to the place and will even manage the social aspects of the work, by simply relying on the kind of interaction formula which had in the past already proved to be effective. The mid-initiation period is characterised by conversation and innocent inquiries concerning different aspects of the organisation and the job itself, from those colleagues with whom the trainee works closely. Both the individual and his colleagues try to gather as much information about one another as possible. It is not unusual to see that, during breaks, lunch hours and other informal and social gatherings, it is the newcomer's extent and depth of knowledge and skills which is being subjected to casual inquiry, but his competence and ability to perform the job is not being questioned.

The initiation stage is signified with ritualistic statements such as 'welcome back mate', 'nice to have you with us', and 'where have you been all the time you were needed?'. These supportive interactions will soon cease and normal daily interaction will be restored. At this stage a false sense of security is prevalent. The individual involved may even reflect on the events of the recent past and will feel proud and delighted that he has handled the situation expertly.

A complete newcomer may even begin to think that the new workplace is very similar to the previous one. It is often thought that the previously learnt social and technical knowledge, skills, attitudes and values are adequate for coping with the present situation. When confronted with change, it is normal to experience 'denial' and to carry on with thinking that really nothing has changed at all. However, all too soon the individual will be reminded that all is not well.

Negotiation This phase is about learning to cope with the new reality that the individual finds himself in. The reason being that unlike the initial experiences, the old social and even task-related skills and knowledge suddenly seem not to guarantee the effectiveness which is expected from the newcomer or the trained employee. Of course, in the position of a newcomer the situation is even worse. Comments such as 'now that you are going to be with us for good, better do things this way', are not uncommon. The early comments and criticisms are usually directed at the individual's performance and often take humorous forms. In this way the individual is given still another chance to learn the values and norms of the operation and conduct in the new workplace.

A trainee manager recalled how he was told by his colleagues that he should 'take it easy, otherwise soon there won't be an office big enough for him and his new ideas'. Criticism as well as approval from colleagues and work mates provides the guidance necessary for the newcomer or trainee to 'learn the ropes' or to adjust his effort and performance accordingly. However, if he insists on 'showing off' his task-related knowledge and skills, sooner than would have been expected, non cooperation and even sabotage will follow.

The feeling that this - new - place is not the same as the previous one or that 'it has considerably changed' will bring with it the burden of depression and ineffectiveness. Naturally, at this stage, the transfer of the task-related aspects of the job will prove to be marginal, simply because the individual has to spend more time learning how to work with others than actually doing the work. As one experienced operative put it, 'if people take a liking to you, you're saved, otherwise God help you'. A tip for the newcomer is to remain a 'learner' and not to attempt to compete with his well socialised and established colleagues too soon.

For the manager, the advice is not to expect too much, too soon. Often, many weeks are needed to overcome the negotiation phase and its learning processes. It is at this crucial phase of socialisation that the individual trainee or the retrained employee needs to be given ample support, especially from their superiors and those in charge. The individual ought to be provided with 'coaching' and if necessary, either formally or informally should be 'adopted' by a senior member of staff in order that he may survive the inevitable period of depression and having to 'facing up' to the new reality.

The extent of the rejection or acceptance which is experienced by the individual from his peers and colleagues and the amount of support received from his superiors and bosses, in the main determines the limit to which the individual will be able to display the newly acquired socio-technical knowledge and skills. Observation has shown how, in some situations, the 'ineffectiveness' associated with the negotiation phase is taken as a permanent facet of the individual's attitude to work and therefore, either the 'training' is blamed for not being transferable or the individual concerned is classed as not being able to 'fit in' and accordingly sent to 'Coventry', transferred or even dismissed.

Integration Should the employee or trainee survive the depression period and manage to successfully negotiate the new reality, the recovery phase begins. Although, still, by and large ineffective, from time to time the individual uses the process of trial and error to test the newly learnt skills, knowledge and values. Again, the support which is received from colleagues, peers and superiors is vital to the completion of the recovery stage. If the individual has been successful in his attempts to become accepted by his immediate work mates or colleagues, the trust which is then placed in him by a few, prompts others to see him as 'alright', and as 'doing fine' or even as 'coming along' nicely.

If, however, the individual withstands the pressures to learn how to operate in the new job, based on the new values, rules and regulations, the second wave of resistance will be generated through the social system. This time it will be strong enough to completely reject the newly transplanted person from the workplace. Comments such as 'he should have known better than to...', 'after twelve months still...', 'when is he going to learn?' and 'let's face it we made a mistake, he hasn't got it in him' will usually mark the beginning of the rejection process. This is followed by depriving the individual of access to resources and maybe even ostracism. The latter behaviours are indicative of the feeling that the trainee will not be tolerated any longer. However, the individual trainee who has relearnt the ways and means of how to get the job done without 'stepping on other peoples toes' soon gains confidence and becomes effective.

It is vital to remember, that becoming effective and being accepted by the organisational social system does not necessarily mean that transfer has positively taken place. In many cases the trainee, for the sake of enjoying a trouble free work relationship and the restoration of peace at work, will have to give in to the implicit and explicit demands which are made of him concerning his task and the socially related aspects of his job. Thus, under pressure he decides to conform to the prevailing norms and attitudes.

An experienced consultant, who returned to his organisation after a two year Sabbatical, which he initially regarded as the 'best training he had ever had', discovered that there was no support for his - although proven elsewhere to be effective - new ideas and ways of operating. The harder he tried, the harder he fell and after a short period he had to resign. His colleagues and peers were all in agreement that 'he is capable, exceptionally bright and that he has gained a lot of experience during the last two years', yet the support needed during the negotiation phase was not forth coming. The Director of the organisation, in his seemingly sympathetic manner (quiet voice) commented on how he had to accept his resignation because he 'couldn't understand why he can't fit back into his department'.

Those who survive the transition phases of social learning, will go on to perfect the acquired knowledge and skills and will even be given the opportunity to try out the new and innovative ideas for which they have been formally trained. So long as, it's done collectively and in 'small doses'. The integration of the individual to the organisation becomes complete once the individual becomes a part of the 'whole'. Brown (1965) skilfully discerns, 'Perhaps the simplest way of describing this wholeness is by saying that it is a 'we' feeling; it involves the sort of sympathy and mutual identification for which 'we' is the natural expression. One lives in the feeling of the whole and finds the chief aims of his will in that feeling (P.129).

Smooth or bumpy transition

Whether transition, the social learning obstacle course, takes place smoothly or becomes a bumpy process, depends on the interaction of many factors present within the workplace. The individual's past experience, the type of job for which he is being trained, the methods of training used and the extent of the support provided, all either individually or collectively affect the ways in which transition is managed.

The most important amongst these factors is the method which is to be used for implementing the training. The decision as to whether or not the training should be carried out on-the-job or outside in a centre, has serious implications, as shown here, for the speed and intensity with which the individual trainee has to deal with transition.

In the case of off-the-job training the fact that the trainee is placed in an artificial environment means that most of the task-related learnt knowledge and skills have to be adjusted and altered to meet the standard of performance which is set formally and informally by colleagues, peers and clients when back in the actual work environment. The transition curves in the above case are clearly marked by three distinct initiating, negotiating and integration phases.

Despite the nature of the job, the degree of complexity involved and the extent of the support which is rendered to the individual trainee, the social learning processes have to be completed before one can expect effectiveness and improved performance from the individual concerned. It is not, therefore, unusual to see that transfer in cases where off-the-job methods were utilised is experienced in such low levels when compared with on-the-job types of training.

This is not to suggest that in on-the-job types of training the individual does not experience the change in the workplace. On the contrary, the trainee will experience the same degree of pressure and demands for change from colleagues and peers, but more gradually and stage by stage. Since the trainee, for example an apprentice, is not viewed by his work mates and the boss as a trained individual, their expectation from him , his behaviour and work performance will be adjusted accordingly. Allowance is usually made for a lack of experience and for the fact that 'he is only a learner'. The trainee simultaneously learns to socialise as well as learning to get the job done. Whatever he learns can be employed by him, again with the implicit acceptance from his colleagues and peers that, should he make an error, it is only to be expected of him. As long as the employee can put into practice what he has managed to learn on the job, even though his performance still leaves a lot to be desired, because he is a learner he will be tolerated.

The social learning in situations where the 'sitting with Nelly' training method is used will derive from observing how Nelly negotiates the social reality at work. While in the off-the-job situation, the newcomer has to first identify and then learn and even relearn the dominant value system of the workplace and how it exactly works.

The close network of work relationships which are constructed between the on-the-job trainee and his trainers provides him with an opportunity to learn the social aspects of working in that organisation simultaneously on an informal basis. As one foreman commented,

> There is a double standard in operation when you get the job. First they (colleagues and peers) judge your ability and performance on the basis of what you should already know and how you get things done according to the 'rules'. Unless you truly become a part of the family, the expectations remain the same. So really learning to do the job as others do it, like cutting corners, won't do. You have got to become accepted first.

Personal observation has shown that in cases of both management and operative training, an inhouse or on-the-job training method has resulted in minimising the negative effects of the 'depression' period. People are more likely to 'let go' of their past experiences and values and become a part of the whole. The fact is that, for the trainee or newcomer, there are so many things to be learnt and mostly in connection with the socialisation that it would be almost impossible to expect any formal course of training to incorporate all of it in its content (See Figure 4.1).

While the above generalisation is helpful in most cases. When making a distinction between training situations, based on the proximity to the actual workplace environment, two other factors also need to be included in the analysis. These are;

a) the degree of intensity of the social relearning processes which the individual trainee experiences (high in cases of off-the-job and low in cases of on-the-job) and,

b) the type of job for which the training course has been designed and formulated.

Each form of training, be it a management or operative programme, has its own implications for transition and transfer. This will be dealt with in Chapter Six, where the scope and limitations for adopting a socio-technical approach in order to maximise the transfer of learnt knowledge and skill to the job, are discussed in some detail.

Conclusion

The social learning processes to which all members of the organisation whether a trainee or trained individual are continuously exposed, act as a powerful regulating mechanism throughout the hierarchy of the organisation. Yet, in relation to training and its transfer they only constitute one half of the total learning that has to be done before the trainee becomes effective at work.

The traditional explanation of transfer only accounts for the results of the task-related aspects of a training programme without seriously considering the host of decisive social factors which have been dealt with here under the umbrella of socialisation.

The success or failure of a training programme, therefore, is partially determined by whether the individual trainee can successfully be initiated into the workplace social settings so that he can effectively negotiate the social reality and thus learn what is necessary for his final integration into the socio-technical system of the organisation.

Naturally each phase of transition will be experienced differently by individual trainees. This will be largely determined by the individuals previous degree of exposure to the complex processes and interactions of a host of interrelated factors. Amongst these factors the proximity to the workplace, as a criterion for deciding the use of on or off-the-job methods, is the most influential one, specially when it concerns the creation of a 'smooth' or 'bumpy' process of adjustment to work.

In Chapter Five, based on the above, the construction of the socio-technical model of transfer for explaining the effectiveness of training will be attempted.

5 A socio-technical explanation for transfer of learning

Introduction

To highlight the problematic nature of transfer, within the context of training and development, let's consider the following plausible situation. A typical training programme X, an off-the-job type, is terminated. An end of course evaluation activity has been carried out and a promising result, e.g. that learning has taken place, is expected. Certificates have been awarded and the trainees have gone back to work either to their current position or to a new one and have begun to perform.

The trainers are jubilant that the main objectives of the training programme have been achieved and the organisers of the course are now awaiting the arrival of a 'new batch' of trainees.

At work it is naturally expected that the time for the training to pay off has arrived. However, it is not uncommon to observe that these expectations are dashed and that the investors (management or owners of the organisation) find themselves facing the reality of low or, even worse, ineffective transfer.

From the organisation's point of view, since most of the trainees who had participated in training programme X seem to suffer from similar, if not identical, unsatisfactory performance levels, to blame them all for wasting the organisation's scarce resources would not seem justifiable.

Therefore, this explanation for the ineffective transfer will quickly be ruled out.

After all, 'not all the personnel involved can be thick, can they?' So who is to be blamed for the disappointing results? The decision that the employees required some form of training had been a sound one, and so it must be the training centre which is to be blamed for not enabling the individuals to do their job properly. It is not uncommon for the affected organisation to approach another training centre, in the hope that the results would be different.

This hypothetical situation adequately illustrates the consequences of the adoption of a purely task-related approach to training, the material to be learnt (learning content), the choice and use of a training method and, last but not least, the transfer of learnt material to the job situation.

One of the implications of adopting a predominantly technical approach to training and transfer is that, positive transfer is often expected to occur automatically, as an inevitable consequence of formal learning processes. In this way, the presence of social learning processes within the actual work organisation which are acting as determinant factors in the realisation of effective transfer, as well as ensuring the positive outcome of transfer, are conveniently ignored. Why? Because, the social learning processes do not fit into the scheme which traditionalists use to explain an awkward phenomenon such as transfer.

In this chapter, first some of the main barriers to understanding transfer, as a process, are explored. Then, the main premises for constructing a socio-technical model for the analysis of transfer are explained. In a separate discussion, the main differences between *effective learning* and *effective transfer* are illustrated and a five part taxonomy of training is put forward.

Finally, a comprehensive alternative for the analysis of transfer is offered. Such a framework for the analysis of transfer is not intended to only throw light at 'why' positive transfer does not occur as expected, but is also expected to assist with the understanding of the intricate issues involved and ultimately to pave the way for initiating effective transfer.

Task-related transfer: a partial explanation

The existing explanations for transfer, why it doesn't normally occur as expected and how and by what means it can be facilitated, evolves around the theme of the 'task' or the 'role' which a learner (and not necessarily a

101

trainee) is expected to perform at work. Briefly, the transfer of learning (traditionally emphasis is placed on learning and not necessarily on training) is viewed as positive when the learning which has taken place in one situation can be applied or reproduced in another. The course of learning primarily concerns a task of some kind. For example, learning to bore holes in metal sheet, operating a keyboard, handling semi-automatic machinery and the like (Duncan & Kelly, 1983).

If the learning which has taken place in one situation can help the occurrence of other skills or the use of knowledge or attitude elsewhere, then the transfer of learning is referred to as *Vertical* (Glueck, 1974). For example, learning physics can in a generalised way facilitate the process of repairing electrical equipment, the acquisition of knowledge and skills about the principles of combustion engines will enable the learner to understand the working of most engines or the possession a first degree in mechanical engineering can provide the individual with the background principles necessary to recognise the differences in two designs of the same mechnical equipment. In the field of management training, acquiring an indepth knowledge of effective communication is believed to help managers, in a general way, to counsel their employees more effectively.

Transfer is referred to as *Lateral* when specific learnt knowledge or skills results in the carrying out of a specific task (see Chapters One and Three where the use of simulators was discussed). Emphasis is usually placed on the presence of 'identical elements' between the components of learning in one situation and the components of the job in another (McGhee & Thayer, 1961; Stammer and Patrick, 1975; Annett, 1983). The use of Flight Simulators for training pilots is probably the most well known example of the application of this principle for achieving a higher (not ultimate) transfer of learning.

Finally, transfer is referred to as *Negative* when the learning which has already taken place elsewhere will in a negative way hinder or prohibit the learning of new knowledge, skills or even behaviour and attitudes (Holding, 1965; Duncan & Kelly, 1983; Analoui, 1990). Basically, the core of the argument is based on the interference between two or more established patterns of behaviours which are incompatible with one another. It is usually the norm to advise the learner to go through a process of 'undoing' prior to embarking upon the task of learning the new skills or different patterns of behaviour.

In a nutshell, what the above theories offer is an explanation of how the task-related learning aspect of a training situation can be transferred to the actual workplace. The explanations offered for transfer have been primarily of a psychological nature, rather than a socio-psychological one.

Traditionally, the workplace organisation has not been viewed as a dynamic learning situation, thus rarely have the effects of learning, including the socialisation processes, which usually take place within the organisation, been analysed or considered as having a substantial impact on the present learning processes, previously acquired learning or the future transfer of the previously learnt materials.

The task-related approach towards understanding or explaining the phenomenon of transfer has been largely influenced by the orthodox perspective adopted by managers, trainers, writers and theorists alike, when the role of people in work organisations, training situations and the role of the organisation in the daily life of people, has been discussed. When increased productivity becomes the main preoccupation, it is not surprising to see that *getting the job done* becomes the main concern for practitioners. Trainers, in a mechanical way, are then held responsible for programming people as though they are mere machines, albeit a sophisticated one.

The outcome of adopting the mechanistic approach to transfer and of sending the employee away to a training centre with the expectation that he or she will virtually be fitted with the desired knowledge and skills, is often a disappointing one. It is difficult to guarantee that effective learning will take place as expected, let alone the occurrence of it's positive transfer on the employee's return to work. Unfortunately, the literature on training supports the misunderstood conception that:

a) Training and learning are interrelated processes, but that the learning is of the task-related material and the transfer of training is nothing but the transfer to the workplace of the learning which was carried out earlier. It is inconceivable for traditionalists to consider that in practice the relatively small amount of learning which has taken place in a training centre may not, for organisational reasons, be transferred to the job.

b) Training methods are ways (means) by which people are taught certain skills, knowledge, behaviours and attitudes. The emphasis should be placed on the active role of the trainers, in their position as controllers of learning situations. It is assumed that the trainees ought to be regarded as passive acquirers of knowledge and skills, who are helpless to identify and generally manage their own learning.

The effectiveness of the training methods used is assessed based on the extent to which they enable the individual trainee to perform a task, rather than the degree to which they are enabled to become an effective member of the organisation. The fact is that on-the-job methods have been observed to facilitate learning and the positive transfer of that learning is not considered as having had anything to do with the social learning processes which people undergo simultaneously in the workplace and which are an indispensable aspect of effective performance.

c) When the question of how transfer can be facilitated is considered, it is generally argued that attention must be paid to those known factors which act as motivators for reinforcing, enhancing and facilitating the learning processes rather than their transfer to the job. Moreover, the learning, by and large, does not include the social learning activities which occur within the workplace. It is not unusual, therefore, to see that the motivation offered to the individual trainees ceases as soon as it becomes evident that the task-related aspect of the learning has been successfully completed.

The underlying philosophy of this task-related approach to training and transfer is at best partial and at its worst a simplistic one. It deals with the issues of learning and training in a dichotomous manner.

Analysis of the various training modes and methods which are currently being employed in industry and the assessment of their potential for effective transfer has led to the discovery that, there appears to be a correlation between the proximity of the training location, in relation to the actual workplace, and the degree of effective transfer of the learnt material knowledge and skills to the job. (See Figure 5.1.)

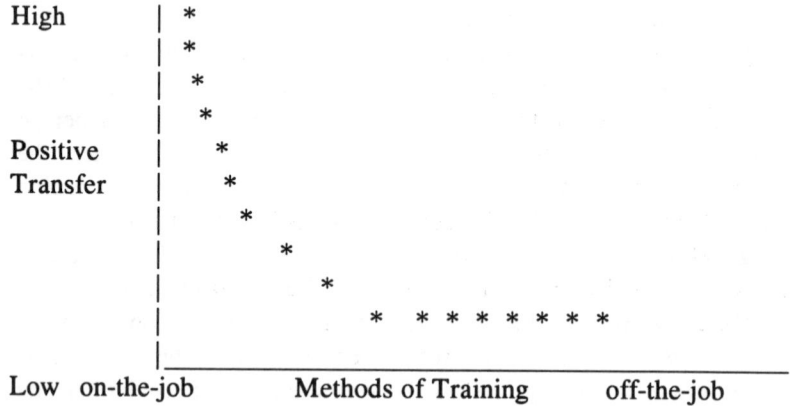

Figure 5.1 The observed degree of effective transfer and its relationship with the proximity of the training methods to the actual workplace

The conclusion reached is that the actual workplace or 'the end of the line', as it is commonly referred to by training instructors, plays a determinant and decisive role in either 'making or breaking' the objectives pursued by training programmes.

Moreover, the actual workplace ought to be viewed, as what it really is, a dynamic learning environment, where individuals including trainees are inevitably exposed to socialisation processes, amongst other things, albeit often in indirect and implicit ways. The subscribers to traditionally task-related focussed explanations for transfer, to a lesser or greater degree, fail to consider the impact of the inescapable socio-psychological 'transition processes' on the dynamics of the realisation of the acquired knowledge, skills and attitudes on the job.

The socio-technical approach

In order to demonstrate the significance of the role of the actual workplace in training and ultimately its impact on the realisation of transfer either in positive or negative terms, it is purported here that a clear distinction must be made between the technical and social learning aspects of training.

a) Technical learning processes are those which tend to evolve around the acquisition of the role-related knowledge and skills which are necessary to perform a task satisfactorily.

b) Social learning processes are those concerned with understanding the constituent elements of the social structure of the workplace. For example, how to maintain group membership, how to meet others expectations and more importantly how to perform a task according to the established patterns of rules and regulations as well as the prevailing norms and beliefs of the workplace.

In this way the behaviour of individuals in the actual workplace is viewed as consisting of socio-technical properties for which the necessary training has to be provided. In order that the reader can fully appreciate the significance of the above distinction for understanding the dynamics of transfer, the following analogy originally used by Brown (1965) has been borrowed.

Brown contends that;

> The action of a coal miner when drilling a hole in which he places an explosive charge is strictly technical...whereas his social behaviour [being engaged in conversation with workmates and

attending union meetings] belongs to the informal structure of the organisation (p.131).

Hyman (1972) reminds us of the case of miners in a colliery in England who abided by an informally agreed upon rule which was religiously enforced and adhered to by all members of the team, that should a team member feel unwell he should take a day off. This rule was established to safeguard the safety of the other members in a situation where individual team members are expected to show care and consideration for the survival and well being of the group as a whole.

In on-the-job training situations these two sets of learning processes, the task and social-related components of the training tend to overlap considerably. Thus, as observed, the closer the training situation is to the actual workplace, the greater are the trainee's opportunities for becoming exposed to or familiarised with the social skills and knowledge required.

As shown in Chapter Four, where the topic of transition was discussed, in an on-the-job training situation the process of the integration of an individual into the reality of the workplace is facilitated because the trainee is learning to do a job in the job-related social community of the workplace.

Most writers and theorists in the field of training   agree that on-the-job training is most suitable for learning tasks of low complexity, yet they find it difficult to provide a rational explanation - other than stating that tasks of low complexity require less concentration - for facilitated transfer. The socio-technical view of transfer, on the other hand, enables us to see why the trainee has to undertake both the learning of technical - i.e. learning material of low complexity - and social aspects of work - operating social norms and values prevalent in the workplace - almost simultaneously.

In fact, learning tends to occur concurrently at two distinguishable levels. In the case of tasks of low complexity, the less demanding nature of the technical aspect of the learning to perform that task provides the trainee with ample time and opportunity for interaction with others and to learn the social aspects of the work. Practitioners, however, who are primarily concerned with the job-related performance may not see, or value, the social learning processes in which the individual trainee will be involved while training on-the-job. Thus, it is not unusual to see that the significance of learning the social aspects of the job for improved productivity and efficiency of the trainee is generally taken for granted.

If, however, in an on-the-job situation, the nature of the task to be learnt is of a complex nature, not only will the distraction caused by the operations or services of the organisation interfere with effective learning, but the demanding nature of the technical learning would also considerably limit the individual learner from taking on board the second series of learning processes, which are probably even more influential on his prolonged performance in the organisation than the purely task-related aspects.

Observations made in industry also indicate that the lower the complexity of the task to be performed - manual or semi-skilled job - the higher the intensity of the social interactions amongst the operatives (see Figure 5.2).

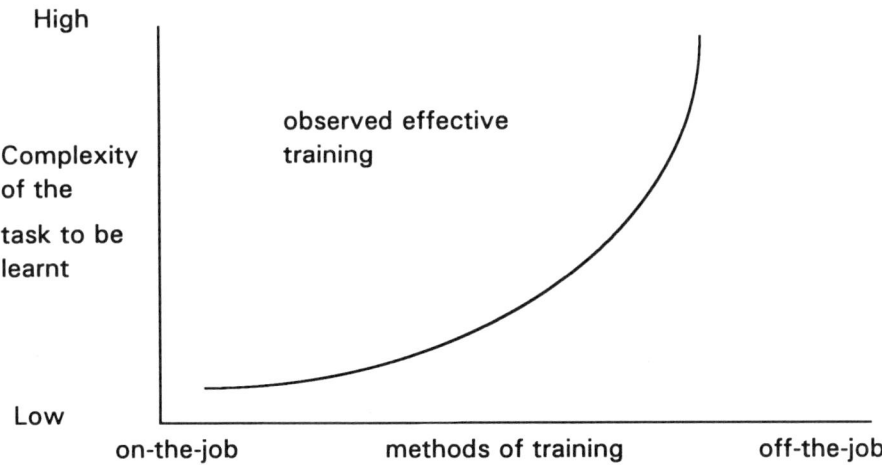

Figure 5.2   The inverse relationship between the complexity of the task to be learnt and the proximity of the method to the actual workplace

The above analogy is also applicable in the field of management training. The lower the position held by the role occupier, for example supervisory (if we accept supervisory roles as the early stages of managerial responsibility) and junior management positions, the greater the degree of intense socialisation and interaction between the role occupiers and their colleagues and peers.

In off-the-job situations, the trainee, having acquired the necessary knowledge and skills, will eventually have to face the social reality of the workplace - a learning programme which is not accounted for by the trainers and instructors and is often unexpected by the trainees involved. As Seymore (1966) states,

> Where the trainees have undergone off-the-job training in a situation, the completion of their training will normally coincide with the transfer to the factory. This for many trainees is a disturbing experience and may give rise to a critical drop in performance or quality (p.98).

A foreman shared his recollections of his early days of working for a processing firm.

> It is clear now, but was not clear then. You walk into the place thinking you know it all, but you really don't. Even if you have only moved one step up and have to work on a different side of the same factory, you've got to do it all over again. Let's face it, the bloke who works next to you has more to say in how you should do the job than the management. If you do not know the job but they [workmates] like you, they'll teach you, cover for you. You name it and they will do it for you. But if you can't get on with others, well you are a goner, even if you're a genius.

It can only be concluded that in the majority of situations, if both the processes of technical and social learnings are guaranteed to take place simultaneously, the training and transfer of the learnt material to the job, would undoubtedly be more effective. However, while socialisation processes in on-the-job training tend to facilitate training for tasks of low complexity, the same argument can not be valid for tasks which are of high complexity. One plausible explanation is that effective socialisation may take much longer than expected especially since the learning of the task-related aspects of the job are demanding and require more attention being paid to them. In such situations, one way to minimise the ordeal which the trainee has to face is to plan for initiating the social learning processes while the trainee is still at the training centre.

Stammer and Patrick (1975) also condone the use of supplementary social learning processes. They argue that;

> ...it should not be thought that training [automatically] ends with transfer to the job situation. No matter how high the level of fidelity

of simulation, it should, where possible, be followed by some on-the-job training or supervision (1975, p.100).

Unfortunately, like countless other writers on the subject, their accounts of the social and technical learning aspects of training to perform a job neither identifies nor distinguishes one from the other, nor are they considered in terms of their impact on the final realisation of effective transfer to the job.

Text books on training and development, as shown in the above example, by and large, do not provide an adequate account of the socio-technical analysis of training needs. The explanations given usually go no further than considering the effects of the physical properties - the most visible to the naked eye - of the work environment on trainees and their learning capabilities. That is, the amount of disturbance caused by noise, smell and similar distractions associated with the workplace (Gleuck, 1977). In many cases reference is made to the presence of 'identical elements' (Ellis, 1965) and the significance of 'concept learning' (Shivers, 1980), 'knowledge of results' (Holding, 1965), and the use of other facilitators for learning. Predominantly the stress is placed on the *recollection of learnt materials* rather than providing adequate explanation concerning the process of the socio-technical dynamics of the 'transfer of learning' to the actual workplace and the illumination of problems, which are often of a social nature rather than a technical one.

Effective learning

Admittedly, training and transfer are interrelated issues, but the literature which is available on training, especially that which concerns the learning aspects, do not make a clear distinction between 'effective learning' and 'effective transfer'. Often the need to make a distinction between effective training and transfer is conveniently overlooked and it is simply argued that training is more effective if off-the-job programmes are employed for tasks of a complex nature.

Moreover, it is safely but erroneously assumed that transfer is mostly about the carrying over of the learnt task-related aspects of the job and has little to do with the social activities of the workplace. Therefore, unintentionally the extent and impact of other learning processes to which the trainee becomes exposed, though mostly in an unstructured and unplanned way is grossly understated. It must be stressed here that the

109

relationship between the complexity of the task content and the degree of proximity of the training location to the actual workplace, tends to inversely affect the degree of effective learning but not necessarily the degree of the effective transfer to the job. Bearing in mind that recollection of what is learnt, though important, only partially affects the process of effective transfer. That is only in situations when the 'doing' aspect of the job can benefit from remembering what has previously been learnt elsewhere. (See Figure 5.3).

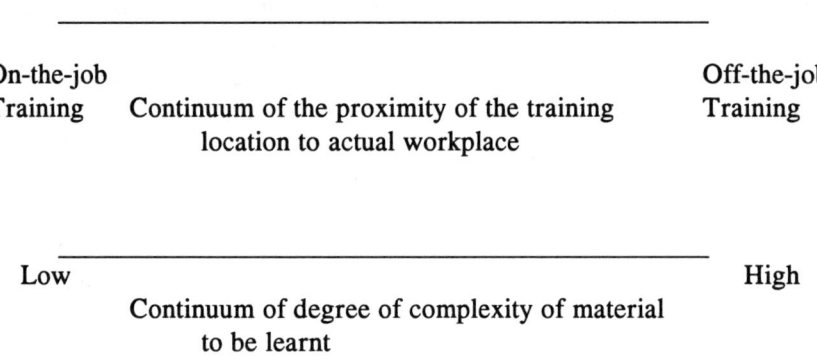

Figure 5.3   The relationship between the social and technical complexity of the learning processes involved and an effective degree of learning

Does socialisation and its related learning processes have no effect on the task-related content of a job, especially in an off-the-job training situation? How do the socio-technical perspectives account for the occurrence of learning processes in such situations? The answer to the above is a simple one; socialisation, occurs in varying degrees and intensity, wherever people interact with one another. But does it have an effect on the effectiveness of the learning and ultimately the transfer?

In the same way that individual trainees or recruits begin to socialise with others and begin to learn the standards of performance and conduct in the workplace, the trainee and learner who share a learning situation, in, for example a training centre, will also almost immediately commence the learning of the primary group norms and values.

It has been observed that even at this stage, effective learning can only

110

be guaranteed if the trainers involved can successfully socialise the learners and obtain a fair degree of integration amongst the individual trainees involved. Trainers and educators are generally aware of the need for a 'match' or for creating a balance between the various sets of factors or learning processes to which the trainees are exposed. These are usually referred to as the 'pressures which are felt by the trainees' whilst involved in learning situations of one sort or another.

As a rule, in almost any kind of training situation a balance between the social and the purely role-related aspects of the job determines the degree of effectiveness in terms of acquiring relevant knowledge and skills on the part of the trainees involved. This balance between the social and technical aspects of learning can be diagrammatically illustrated as below (see Figure 5.4).

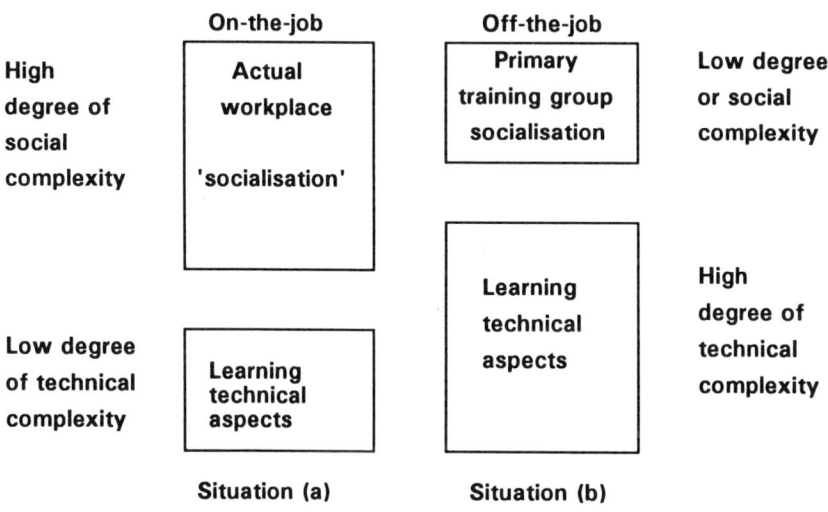

Figure 5.4 The balance between the social and the technical complexity of the learning processes involved and the effective degree of learning

The above model illustrates why it is the case that tasks of low complexity are generally learnt with considerably more ease in an on-the-job situation, than tasks of a elaborate nature. As shown in Fig 5.4 the hypothetical trainee X reaches the peak of his effective learning at either extreme, simply because the aggregate of the amount of pressures resulting from undergoing two different types of learnings are more or less equal in either situation. In situation (b) the technical pressures which derive from the complexities of the material to be learnt are greater than the social skills and knowledge required to socialise effectively at the primary level in training centre.

Primary socialisation and effective learning: a case

In a well known training centre, the duration of the management courses which were offered to senior managers, on an off-the-job basis, amounted to twelve weeks. The residential nature of these courses meant that participants experienced socialisation, although at the primary level, both inside the centre and outside of it in their residential quarters. It was observed that as the weeks went by, some working groups were formed naturally. The members of these small cohesive groups showed a tendency to learn best while operating within the group membership.

Customarily, those trainers who strongly favoured participatory methods for learning managerial concepts asked the trainees at the beginning of a session to form a small group, with the membership of their choice. The the participants were given a relevant task, such as a simulated learning exercise, an actual case study or a role play activity and were subsequently asked to complete the work within the given time limit. Meanwhile, the trainers involved played a passive role and only interfered when they were asked to do so. The main role for the trainers was that of observer and to occasionally act as resource person. Almost all such trainers and educators claimed that, those management trainees who got on well with each other also showed a tendency to learn faster than those who didn't.

Moreover, it was also apparent that the participant trainees who shared a specific cultural background, beliefs and value system or those who happened to be employed within the same ministry, back in their home country, tended to form their groups more quickly and to get on with the task almost immediately.

The trainers, however, who did not benefit from a socio-psychological formal education, background and/or previous experience tended to deliberately separate members of these naturally formed groups, mistakenly believing that this would motivate the trainees to learn more quickly and more effectively.

When approaching the affected participants they revealed that, in the learning situation, the incompatibility between one individual and other members of the group resulted in the group as a whole experiencing difficulty in effectively communicating and relating to one another. Not surprisingly, this often led to the emergence of misunderstandings and conflict, and to the group spending substantial amounts of time in resolving conflicts amongst the group members. The intensified nature of the social learning processes present, for which no allowances were made in terms of time and resources, often meant that the individuals involved had to respond to the social pressures first. Thus, they were obliged to create and agree upon some basic norms and values which they felt were necessary in order to be able to work with one another, before actually become effectively engaged in the task in hand.

Some sponsoring organisations which send a group of trainees rather than an isolated individual to participate on long term residential courses asked for specific group learning activities for their employees while at the centre. These group activities facilitated the process of integration of the members and accelerated the process of primary group socialisation. The ex-post evaluations revealed that the individual members of the above groups showed an improved performance both when at the centre and 'back home' in their actual workplace.

To conclude, in both training modes, on and off-the-job situations, the degree to which effective learning can be achieved in terms of the inverse relationships present between the degree of complexity of the social learning processes and those of a task-related nature.

Transfer of learning in a socio-technical context

Since the problematic nature of transfer is commonly associated with the use of off-the-job training methods, in the following analysis this mode of training will be used to show an extreme case example which epitomises the various learning processes involved. As stated in the above case study, having achieved the correct balance between the social and technical requirements of a training programme, it can then be safely claimed that an effective level of learning is likely to be reached. However, the difficulty arises when the transfer of this learnt material to the actual work situation is unexpectedly retarded.

In order to comprehend the complex and delicate mechanisms involved, the critical stages of the transfer situation in both an on and an off-the-job

113

situation will be closely examined.

On-the-job situation

In an on-the-job training situation, which has been found to be most effective for tasks of low complexity, the fact that the individual trainee is exposed to both workplace socialisation and the role-related learning processes, ensures a gradual process of transfer of learnt knowledge and skills to the job. Although the actual level of observed transfer may fluctuate from one day to another, nevertheless the continuous and uninterrupted involvement of the trainee in the socialisation processes at work means that the individual's progress must have been constantly monitored by others and he has been successfully navigated towards the achievement of the training objectives.

To an observer, effective task-related learning and reasonable transfer does occur simultaneously and, therefore, as Miner (1969) remarks, 'the problem of transition seems to be non-existent'.

Off-the-job situation

In an off-the-job training situation, whether designed for the *operative* or *management* cadre, the process of transfer is not as straight forward as could be expected. The higher level of complexity of the task-related materials to be learnt and the delicate skills to be acquired, necessitates the separation of the trainee from the actual workplace community. This is usually done for reasons such as avoiding disturbance to the normal operations and service of the organisation and for many other reasons which have been dealt with before.

In a training centre, whether in a classroom or in a workshop situation, typically the trainee commences with the primary set of socialisation processes. These social learning activities, as stated earlier, are vital to the successful integration of the individual into the social community. These activities are embodied within the social interactions which routinely take place between the trainee and other members of his primary group.

The intriguing factor, usually observable only to serious and experienced trainers, is that at this point the kind of primary socialisation which is occurring in the centre may act as a motivational and *facilitative* factor in so far as effective learning is concerned. Thus, providing a correct and compatible social mixture of participants is obtained, the socialisation processes will act as a facilitative factor speeding up the process of acquiring the technical learning.

The social skills and knowledge acquired at the primary level within the training centre will also be carried over to the actual workplace. However, the socialisation factors, which in the centre, acted as a facilitative agent and thus have accelerated the process of technical learning, may not necessarily be congruent with the existing value structure, norms and expectations which are prevalent in the workplace. Unavoidably, as is often the case, they may now become a hindrance in the path of the trainee's effective socialisation with his colleagues and workmates in the actual work organisation.

The occurrence of the reverse version of the above scenario is not uncommon either. The incompatibility of the trainee's values and beliefs with the dominant value structure of the primary group at the centre can easily result in the creation of what is often referred to as a 'bad atmosphere' in the learning situation. In turn this mismatch of values and beliefs can act as a non-motivational factor or even as an *inhibitive* agent (as I term it here) and may result in a slowing down of the learning processes, both the social and the technical ones.

On returning to work, the trainee who has experienced ineffective primary socialisation and has therefore not gained a reasonable amount of task-related knowledge, skills and attitudes, which of course was the main reason for his attendance at the training centre, will now face not only a low level of task-related performance but will also suffer from an inability to respond to the social demands and expectations which will be directed at him.

Trainees who bring back from the learning centre less than desirable experiences, may consciously and even unconsciously feel uneasy about either recalling or putting into practice what they have learnt at the training centre. The activities at the training centre become directly associated with negative social interactions at work, thus acting as a factor which inhibits transfer from taking place freely.

The temporary nature of the off-the-job training course also acts as an additional problem, in that the trainees do not feel that it is imperative to deal with any of the expectations of their fellow trainees which they may consider unreasonable. The commitment to deal with individual differences and preferences may not be so great, simply because as one manager commented, 'it will all be over soon'.

On the contrary, in the actual workplace the very fact that the people with whom the trainee works may become permanent influencing factors and may even share the same organisational stage with him, may be all the motivation which is needed to embark upon the realisation process of give and take. The reality of the workplace then becomes negotiable. No matter how powerful the process may be, the outcome will act as a reinforcement whenever the trainee and his colleagues interact with one another on a primary social or socio-technical basis. Thus, increasing the chance of effective learning and successful integration into the system.

Therefore, it becomes evident why it is that the problem of the transfer of training is particularly concerned with the modes of training which take the trainee away from the actual workplace. This is commonly referred to as a *headache* by trainers and practitioners in industry, and is one which has been experienced by many training instructors and specialists in the training industry as a whole.

Infact there are two distinct aspects to this problem. That is, assuming a reasonably effective level of task-related learning has been achieved, the main questions faced are:-

a) Why is it that on many occasions the material which has been effectively learnt at the training centre is not transferred to the actual workplace as expected? and,

b) How and by what means can effective transfer to the actual workplace be guaranteed?

It is believed that a socio-technical framework will provide a more realistic explanation as to why on entering or re-entering the actual workplace, positive or negative transfer may be experienced.

Here, the intricate socio-technical processes involved in the process of transfer will be examined in the context of two separate training situations:-

a) Where, in a training situation, because inadequate attention has been paid to the combined social and technical aspects of a training programme, the result has been trainees which have experienced negative or ineffective transfer; and,

b) Where, in a training situation, a correct balance between the social and technical requirements of a training programme has led to the achievement of positive transfer.

Positive transfer

Figure 5.5 represents the journey that an individual trainee X has to take through a transfer route, from the training centre to the actual workplace. To begin with, X commences with a certain amount of previously acquired social and technical knowledge, skills values and beliefs which have proven to work before.

At the training centre, X is confronted by two sets of learning activities. One is the technical learning, which is aimed at fulfilling the identified role-related performance gap between the present level of his performance and what is often referred to as the 'desired' level of performance expected from him in the future. The technical strand of the learning process is often of an explicit and overt nature. In the course programme, the content pages, usually outline what it is expected that X will learn.

Whether or not effective learning can, at this stage, take place will depend on an assortment of factors. To mention a few, the correct identification of the task-related aspects of the individual's training needs, the relevance of the content to the task for which he is being trained, the degree of structure and expected level of involvement from the individual in the course activities, the length of the course, the nature of the motivation built into the programme, the trainee's own commitment and attitude and finally the trainers' attitudes towards trainees and training as a whole.

However, individual X simultaneously becomes involved in another set of learning activities, which is of a more implicit nature and is often taken for granted. This subtle and covert course of learning commences with the first interaction of individual X with other members of his primary group. At this stage, as shown earlier, the degree of compatibility between X's dominant value and belief schema, and those of the other group members' dominant value structure, essentially determines the degree of:-
a) overall success or failure of the individual in terms of becoming accepted or respected by the primary group community; and
b) the amount of unlearning, re-learning or new learning that X has to do in order to gain and maintain group membership.

The process of socialisation which takes place at the primary level within the centre is rather different from that which X will be confronted with when the programme is completed and he has to go back to work. Because there does not exist an already established value system for the group, members have to actively participate in group activities and gradually create the essential rules, regulations and norms of behaviour necessary for smooth interaction amongst the group members.

Each member of the group, will have to experience a 'mini-transition' period (see Chapter Four) which if not handled properly by the team leader and trainers involved will definitely lead to trainee X not becoming fully integrated into the primary informal social system of the training centre. Ineffective social learning on the part of X at this stage will act as an *inhibitive* factor thus impeding his progress in effectively acquiring the technical aspects of the programme. Successfully constructed social interactions at the training centre, in turn can act as a *facilitative* factor, thus enhancing the process of acquiring task-related knowledge, skills and competences for which the individual has been sent to the centre.

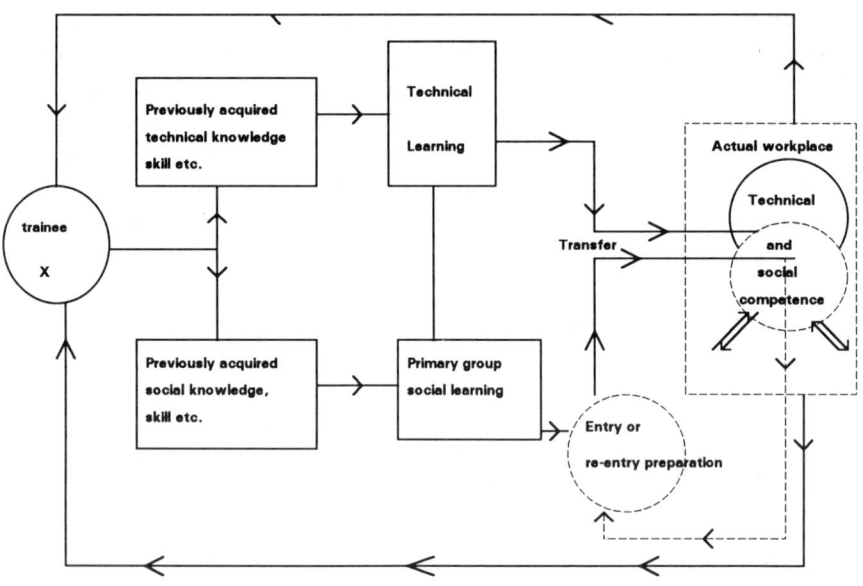

Figure 5.5   Occurrence of the effective (positive) transfer in the context of socio-technical learning, in situation (B)

Depending on the presence of a variety of interrelating factors, such as the duration of the course, size of the group, intensity of the social and technical aspects of the task and most of all the cognitive capability of the individual involved, trainee X gradually begins to learn to make adjustments to or even change his dominant value system to one which is compatible with that of his new technically determined role. Since the main reason for choosing an off-the-job training method had probably been based on the criterion of making the learning of the complex task-related

118

aspects of the job easier and certainly not the facilitation of the socialisation aspects of the trainees job, the technical aspects of the training programme will be taken more seriously and naturally more time and resources will be allocated to such activities.

Providing effective learning has taken place at the centre - that is the trainee has survived the ordeal of the social and technical activities of the training centre primary group - individual X will be moved to the actual workplace. At the workplace, while attempting to demonstrate the newly acquired technical knowledge and skills, which may require some adjustment to new technology other than that which was in use in the training centre and generally transferring the 'learnt' material and skills into a 'doing' state, the individual finds himself in an entirely different social structure and naturally faces new problems which need to be negotiated and ultimately resolved.

If the individual trainee has not been adequately prepared to meet the social requirements of the actual workplace prior to re-entry, the incompatibility of the informal value system with that of the dominant work culture in the workplace, will inevitably result in additional initial ambiguity, confusion and anxiety which if often experienced at the entry stage. The 'lumpy' nature of transition to the new work environment means that the trained individual will initially have to concentrate on surviving the social assault course, never mind finding an opportunity to demonstrate his improved performance.

The second phase of socialisation which was identified earlier, requires a great deal of learning of new things as well as detachment from the old and ineffective values. This will act, at least initially, as an *inhibitive* factor for the realisation of the transfer of the task-related competences of the individuals involved. Under such circumstances, the technical aspects of the individual's overall performance will suffer because of a lack of the necessary understanding and insight about the workplace and its members value system.

As one training consultant humorously put it;

> The introduction of the trainee from the off-the-job learning centre to the actual workplace is like adding thickening to the gravy. If the thickening is not added carefully or the liquid is too hot, one gets a very lumpy and low quality gravy.

An operator recollected the difficulties that he initially faced at the workplace as a result of acquiring incompatible learning experiences at the training centre.

> If you make a mistake. then, you don't just learn from it, you got to live with it. Mistakes cost money. The line manager doesn't like it and your mates won't be happy with you. Why? Because, they lose their productivity bonus and then you feel bad about yourself for acting so stupid in front of others. You certainly won't get a pat on the back, as you would probably have done in the Hall (training centre). Nobody comes to you and politely tells you to try it again. There [on-the-job] you either get it right or put up with the gaffer screaming blue murder.

How can positive transfer be achieved?

Figure 5.6 is intended to illustrate how a socio-technical approach to off-the-job training may result in the achievement of more effective transfer. As shown here the necessary requirements for securing the above objective is first to make sure that an effective level of learning of the task-related aspects of the job has taken place. Unfortunately, as it will be demonstrated in more detail in the next chapter, in most cases it is automatically assumed that the presence of the individual in a learning situation means learning will occur. This, however, may be nothing but gross optimism the part of the employer and trainers concerned.

Many practitioners from industry have commented that they have become increasingly dismayed with the projected image of training centres. It is becoming evident that, after all, training centres may not be the right place for effective learning, even for the acquisition of complex knowledge and skills. Moreover, since the primary socialisation experienced by the trainee while at the centre will undoubtedly have an effect on the extent of the trainee's technical learning, effective task-related learning on his part can not be guaranteed unless the trainee's capacity for socially adjusting to the other participants is first correctly assessed. Then, through the provision of suitable learning situations and activities, he is enabled to achieve a desired level of social competence which is compatible with his past and consistent with that which will be experienced in his present role.

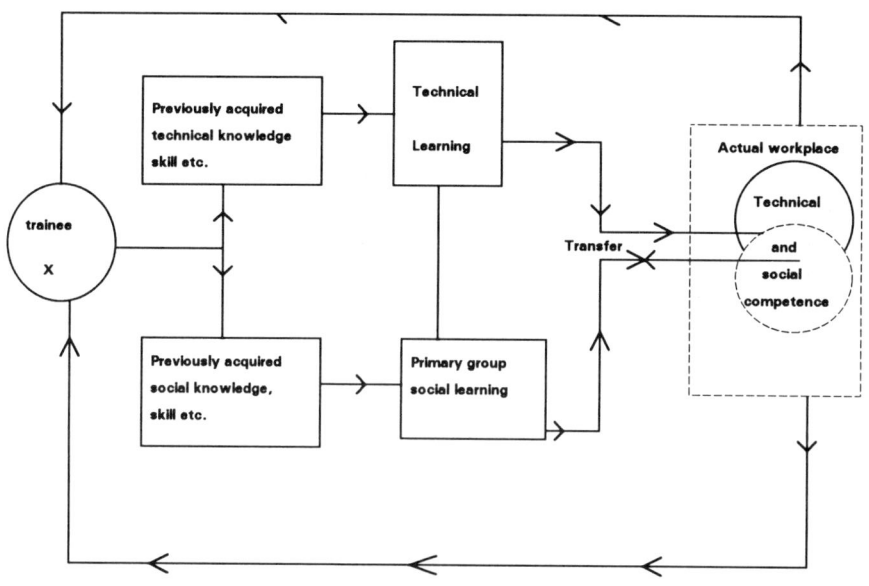

Figure 5.6   The occurrence of the ineffective (negative) transfer in the context of socio-technical learning, in situation (A)

In the training situation, as explained in the previous chapter, where the potential of methods for transfer were discussed, the achievement of effective learning, that is the acquisition of technical skills, knowledge and materials, which is motivated (facilitated) by the presence of a compatible social environment, does not necessarily guarantee the successful transfer of the learnt material of a socio-technical nature to the actual workplace.

It is at this crucial stage - either during or just after the termination of a particular training programme, depending on the specific needs of the situation, that the trainee should be prepared to enter the informal social system of the organisation. This act of entry or re-entry, as the case maybe, must take place in such a way that the least amount of disturbance is caused to the actual workplace and at the same time effort must be made to minimise the inevitable social pressure which are experienced by the trainee when commencing his interaction with others at work.

This necessary activity which needs to be included in any off-the-job training programme is illustrated (see Fig 5.6) and is referred to as the 'entry or re-entry preparation stage'. It is believed that this kind of preparation made prior to entry, will ensure a smooth passage into the organisation and through the transition period in the workplace.

This preparation period will act in a similar way to the 'pressurised tank' which is used by divers, who have to work for long periods at great depths, on their return to the vessel. Naturally, the longer the period of absence from the actual workplace, the longer the period of recovery. The preparation should, of course, include the provision of a realistic vision of what lies ahead of the trainee at work.

At the Development and Project Planning Centre, the University of Bradford, the author has applied the principle of the social technical model to the design of courses for the training of middle and senior project managers from developing countries. The trainees usually stay away from their actual work environment for a period of twelve weeks, on a residential basis. Previously, they had not been adequately prepared for the crucial stage of re-entry into their organisation after training and, amongst other things, they reported that they had experienced a feeling of not understanding why their performance had suffered drastically.

To remedy the above, it was decided that not only did effective socialisation at the primary stage in the centre have to be systematically implemented and included as a major component of the programme and facilitated through participative learning methods and experiences, but also that the twelfth week of the course should be primarily devoted to preparation for re-entry to the workplace.

One aspect of this part of the preparation programme was to familiarise the participants with the principle of transition (see Chapter Four) and with the fact that they should expect some re-learning, once they arrive in their organisations. The follow up assessment, showed that preparation of this kind had undoubtedly helped the smoother completion of the transition period at work and the realisation of reasonable transfer soon after re-entry to the work environment. As one senior manager commented;

> No amount of preparation removes the need for re-learning. In my case, since I had been warned about the 'transition period', at least I could understand why others behaved towards me the way they did and why my performance suffered so much. Certainly during the first half of the year [six months after re-entry to the department], because so much had happened whilst I was away, it took so long to get back into the mainstream of work again.

What serious trainers and practitioners need to remember
preparation for re-entry may prove futile, unless suffici
given by their superiors. This kind of institutional support
for the employee will act as a cushion for softer landing
work. It will facilitate a less troublesome experience of transit
individual involved. It should also help in the case of a newcomer
terms of the adjustment of his expectations from the organisation and its
people thus enhancing the process of the recovery from the ordeal of
physical transfer.

Types of training and socio-technical transfer: a taxonomy

The basic principles utilised in the construction of a socio-technical model
of transfer have primarily derived from the basic distinction which was
made between the modes of training according to their proximity to the
workplace.

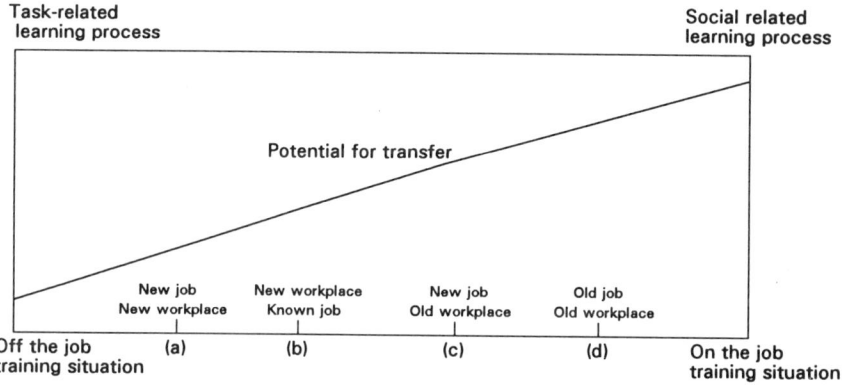

Figure 5.7   A taxonomy of socio-technical model of transfer and types of
training situations

As shown in Figure 5.7   there are two extreme learning situations
identifiable; on one extreme, the off-the-job type which is characterised by
its physical separation from the actual workplace, and on the other, the on-

123

ne-job mode of training which is either close to or located within the actual work environment.

It is evident that inherent in any form of training activity, there is a combination of social and technical learning processes which constitute the total component of the programme. As the training situation comes closer to the actual workplace, the social learning processes begin to accelerate and so is the potential for experiencing effective transfer.

However, when considering the different situations in which the transfer of learning is expected to take place, training methods can also be divided into another four main groups. This taxonomy has been made possible by considering whether or not after the completion of the training the trainee is going to, *a new job in a new workplace, a new workplace but a known job, a new job in an old workplace* or *an old job in an old workplace*. These four identified main types of training forms also have different implications for the adoption of a socio-technical approach to transfer.

A new job in a new workplace

As pointed out earlier, the transfer of the technical knowledge, skills and performance as a whole, is affected by the extent to which an individual possesses the ability and skills to cope with the demands made of him by the social system of the work community. Social interaction within the workplace will act as an inhibitive factor if the new entrant is not prepared for them. As suggested, the minimum requirement is that attempts should be made to adapt the present training programmes (induction or otherwise) to meet the projected social learning needs of the trainee. The social learning processes should be designed specifically to include the social skills which are found to be most relevant to the particular workplace into which the individual is going.

It has been observed that the possession of the relevant ability and skills, on the part of new entrants, to cope with the social demands reduces his chances of being rejected by the informal workplace social community and in effect 'buys' him enough time to become properly acclimatised to the social and technical climate of the job. Often individuals who are not properly socialised into the workplace system tend to feel unwanted and thus become ineffective as a result. Continuous support on the part of peers and colleagues, on the other hand, would facilitate and accelerate the process of becoming a fully fledged member and would result in the enhancement of positive transfer.

Micheal, a well qualified economist joined a medium sized consultancy group with an international reputation. The recruitment committee which comprised of four senior members of the organisation and one administrator 'short listed' Micheal on the strength of his qualifications, work experience, technical knowledge concerning his relevant subject, managerial experience as a project appraiser and his impeccable references which all referred to his technical skills, capabilities and competences. All this impressed the panel, so much so that he was 'given the job'. The lack of an established procedure for socialising new entrants into the company life meant that Micheal was told to 'join the on going training sessions, if he wished to do so, to get the hang of the business'. Micheal who was basically an introvert person and one who incidentally did not agree with the 'ways things were done in the company' soon became disliked and ostracised by the other members of the group. It came to a point that as he put it, 'I could not do anything right'. According to the Director, even his technical expertise and specialisation was being questioned. In a meeting a member of the group whose ways of dealing with infrastructural projects were questioned by Micheal, declared that 'his credentials are phoney. He must go'. Micheal rejected by his colleagues became more and more distant from the social community of the company, was demotivated and his performance began to suffer. He confided in a colleague;

> I've never seen anything like this before. I have done absolutely nothing to upset anyone. I just minded my own business, hoping to be left alone, but to no avail. Such a hostile work environment. But if they hope I will resign, they are barking up the wrong tree. I have a three year contract.

After only two years the increasing pressure on the Director compelled him to ask Micheal to resign. Compensation, in the form of a large sum of money and a good reference was offered to Micheal to persuade him to leave the group 'without trouble'. Micheal now works in a consultancy in the South of England. He described his entry experience as;

> Totally different from that place. From the very beginning I found myself having to participate in the social activities and I was coached by James (an experienced consultant with that group). He took me under his wing, any problems and James helped me to sort

it out, at least in the early stages. I was offered the chance to join an interpersonal skills training course which was organised by the training department. I did and learnt more in that weekend than I had done in the whole two years I spent in the North.

New workplace, known job

When individuals are already familiar with the nature of their particular job, it is usually expected that the transfer of its technical aspects will not pose a serious problem. Indeed, this is so in most cases and once the individual has successfully gone through the 'transition' process, the positive transfer of knowledge, skills and work experience will soon follow.

However, the fact that the individual is already in possession of certain social skills which have been learnt in his previous place of employment can complicate the issue. Observation has shown that where an individual has been exposed to social learning processes in one workplace, these previously learnt social skills will act as either facilitative or inhibitive factors for effective transfer depending on whether or not they are compatible with the dominant social value system (culture) of the new workplace.

If the work culture of the old and new workplaces are incompatible, the individual needs to undergo an 'undoing' exercise of what has previously been learnt and to 'learn' about the informal social system of the new workplace. It is a common misconception that those with years of experience tend to fit more easily into their new jobs and, therefore, require little or no social induction training.

The differences between the cultures of the two workplaces become greatest and most visible in cases where an individual changes job from a public sector organisation to a private enterprise or visa versa. The role culture which characterises the public sector organisations places emphasis on the need for an abundance of rules, regulations, formal communication and the centralisation of power and decision making. Whereas the private sector seems to be more flexible in its attitude to change and the need for promoting informal and two way communication, with fewer rules and procedures in existence. Immersion in one culture makes the process of transition to another extremely difficult even if the nature of the job or role to be performed has remained the same.

126

Susan: the catering manager

Susan joined Leisure Limited in 1980 and like her contemporaries, who benefited from City and Guilds Certificates, Higher National Diplomas and University degrees, she directly joined the management cadre.

The company comprises of several subsidiary enterprises such as public houses, restaurants, bingo halls, fast food outlets and even betting shops, all over mainland Britain, the Middle East and the USA. The company policy has always stressed on periodic transfers from one branch to another, albeit in the same field (business). It is normal for the manager of a night club in Scotland to be told, on short notice, that he or she has to move down to Wales and take over a similar operation there. Susan counted herself as lucky, since over the past ten years continuous employment she had not had to move around too much. 'I suppose they (the bosses) liked my performance and the way I did my job, but it had to happen one day.'

Susan was told that she had to move down to a large city in the heart of Northwest England and take up a similar position as catering manager - though in a much bigger and more glamorous branch. The move to the new work environment, even though it was the same job, was still interpreted by Susan and her colleagues as a 'step up in the right direction'. The benefits of a more generous allowances and being the catering manager of one of the four largest entertainment establishments in the country was regarded as a 'definite promotion'.

The management structure of the new workplace was the same as the previous one, with the General Manager, placed at the top of the two tier organisational hierarchy, being responsible for the whole operation. The catering manager, Susan, was directly accountable to Mr Bond, a retired Major who had joined the company in the 60's.

> I was looking forward to getting my hands on the job. I could hardly wait. Mind you, I was a bit apprehensive about my new colleagues, especially Mr Bond my boss. When I rang him up to say I would be joining him, he asked me to come in the night before my starting date and join the staff meeting which was regularly held at 6.30 p.m. on Wednesdays. I did and boy was that an eye opener.

Tony, the general operations manager, quickly filled me in about how Bond ran the branch. On the night of the meeting, like Tony I stood in the first line, with the staff in rows awaiting the arrival of Mr Bond. It was an unusual experience for me. In my previous job there was a friendly atmosphere. Everyone addressing each other by their first names.

Mr Bond arrived precisely at 6.30 and inspected the staff as though they were a company of soldiers in a barracks. After the meeting I was told to meet him in his office. After one hour waiting he eventually called me in and amongst other things I was told that I should call him *Mr Bond* at all times. I knew then I was heading for trouble... Soon it was like living hell working in that place. No wonder they were loosing so much money. Bond's attitude was atrocious. Everything had to be just precisely as he wanted it and when it came to the stocks no questions could be asked. I was held responsible for 'stolen' stock which was worth hundreds of pounds and I knew that it could not all be due to staff pilferage or wastage.

Till one morning I caught him red handed putting bottles of wine and whisky in the trunk of his Mercedes. I asked Tony what was going on and he nodded his head and said "He is the boss, he can do what he wants, If you want to stay you should put up with it. Besides you haven't seen it all yet". When I confronted Mr Bond and threatened to report him to head office, he in a cool manner said, "It is your word against mine. Do as you are told or I'll make sure there is no career for you in this company. Remember you are my subordinate".

Early in September, about three weeks after her row with the General Manager, Susan received a letter from Head Office telling her that she had to move to the 'Talk of the Village' a small night club in the Northeast. She left the company.

New job at an old workplace

This type of training usually creates the least problems for effective transfer. The employee is already familiar with the dynamics of the workplace's social system and only needs to concentrate on enhancing the task-related aspects of the job or position. However, it must be remembered that in situations where the employee is promoted to a new post which places him in a supervisory or managerial position, previously learnt social-related skills and knowledge may prove inadequate and, therefore, the acquisition of people related skills such as problem solving, conflict resolution, interpersonal communication and so on would be essential in order to guarantee positive transfer.

What is important to bear in mind is that promotion to a senior level does not make the individual more technically capable over night.

Effective transfer could suffer, especially in the area of the task-related aspects of the incumbent's job, when the peer supervisors can expect the new position holder to be able to perform as competently as the person who had previously held this job for a number of years. The social learning process for the new 'promotee' (this term is used here loosely) also includes understanding the expectations of his colleagues from him and being able to see on which aspects of the business the emphasis should be placed. some organisations it was observed that the general understanding, on the part of the peer group and bosses, of the predicaments which a new individual can experience, is shown in terms of providing the trainee with 'a period of grace' in which to 'sort himself out' or 'to find his feet'. This period of re-adjustment ought to be calculated based on the previous degree of competence that the individual had shown in dealing with the new socio-technical expectations and demands which were made of him in his new position.

The probationary period for the new individual also needs to include formal monitoring of his progress. In the words of an experienced executive;

> When an individual is promoted, it is not uncommon to see that he approaches his job with the style and even know how that he used to manage his previous job. Real effectiveness begins when the person learns to treat a new job in a new way.

The bigger the leap an individual experiences in terms of the task-related demands of his new job, the harder he will find it to become socio-technically effective at work.

Headaches for the supervisor

The department store, *Advanced*, like any other reputable store had to fill the vacant positions of those employees who left for other jobs, with either newcomers or employees from their existing personnel. The company policy stated that after a period of three years uninterrupted employment with 'Advanced', shop assistants, depending on their suitability and performance, would become eligible to apply for vacant supervisory or junior management positions.

Depending on the degree of complexity involved and the training needs of the applicants, an induction training programme, either on or off-the-job, would be arranged to enable the applicants to manage the post to which they were promoted. Peter, a junior assistant, had been informed by the management that he had a promising future with the company. Therefore, when a supervisory position became available in the glassware section, he naturally applied for it. Peter knew the ins and outs of working in that section; a bright, ambitious junior employee who could also 'get along' with the staff, especially the other assistants. His previously earned four 'A' levels with good grades made him believe that he had a good chance of getting the job even though he had not gone through the rank and file. For him becoming a supervisor meant that he had to compete with two senior assistants from the same store, though they worked in shoes and cosmetics.

Peter succeeded in securing the supervisory position and was told that he would have to participate in some short courses (twice a month) at a training centre, not far from the store.

After a while, the management described Peter's progress as 'less than desirable'. His immediate boss explained how surprised he was to see a rise in customer complaints;

> Not that he doesn't know the job, he doesn't know how to manage people and I don't just mean the employees (his own previous work mates), but also the customers. I suppose he thought becoming a supervisor meant just more workload, but we haven't given up on him yet.

Peter also had mixed feelings about his own progress. He commented;

> The first three months, I must admit, weren't all that easy. I had to learn to fill in forms and arrange weekly meetings, how to send off orders in time and other things. The fact that I knew everybody that I worked with initially helped, though after a while my own mates started treating me differently. It was when another assistant told me, 'Now you are a part of the management' that it dawned on me that, that was why the staff were being awkward towards me. The new outfit didn't help either. It was difficult to strike the right chord. Being younger than some of them (assistants) meant that at times the older ones wouldn't listen. It was one headache after another. Let's face it, I already knew how to do the paperwork and how to deal with the customers, alright but I had no idea what it was going to be like being a supervisor, especially when it came to dealing with the staff. It was too big a jump for me I suppose.

Peter survived his induction training and the relatively long period of transition, partly because the management were aware of the gap present in his knowledge and skills which he needed to become an effective supervisor and made arrangements for his training in the identified areas relating to his new job. Also, a combination of the fact that he had already had some understanding of how the place 'ticked' together with the support of his immediate boss who helped him 'to pull through'. Peter had underestimated the skills and knowledge required to deal with people and the ability which was needed to manage them as his subordinates. It is ironic but most managers underestimate this vital aspect of their job when moving to a new position.

Old job at an old workplace

Most organisations are involved in this type of training. 'In house' training often proves to be more effective than sending employees away from the organisation, particularly for a long period of time. On-the-job training is usually undertaken as a response to a need for change in one area of the organisation's activities. Employees, are usually provided with an opportunity to bridge the gap between their present performance and what is seen as the new and desirable performance level. In these cases, as shown in Fig 5.7 the individual is already in possession of the social skills and knowledge which are relevant and related to his work, thus only the technical requirements of his job needs to be emphasised.

However, if an internal re-organisation of the working constellations is envisaged or new technology is being introduced which will require employees to establish different patterns of work relationships, the trainees ought to be helped to find their place within the new social system of the workplace. The introduction of team building activities, quality circle, brain-storming and the like would help to strengthen work relationships and therefore enhance the transfer of training.

New computers

A haberdashery suppliers had to eventually update their computers system which was used by all sections, accountants, secretarial, sales, packing and storage departments. Constant complaints from the sales and distribution network meant that the existing '104 system' equipped with 808 micro processing chip had to be replaced with faster, more user friendly and bigger capacity computers for the storage and processing of data. The Board approved their purchase and 64 sets of hardware together with up to date software were installed side by side with the old ones.

The decision to use on-the-job training was an option that had many supporters. The staff were given two hours intensive training sessions on a rota basis for a period of three weeks. The availability of specialists supplied by the computer manufacturers meant that the staff worked with specialists and the technical learning proceeded on a gradual but planned basis.

The Managing Director commented:

> It worked very well for us. Of course, some staff were quicker than others, but they on an informal basis assisted others and gradually everyone's ability levelled out. We did experience some teething difficulties during the change over, but overall it has been very satisfactory. We also decided instead of auctioning off the existing hardware and probably getting very little for it, that we should use them as an incentive for the staff. In this way, once the business was transferred to the new machines we offered the old ones, still good enough to be used as PCs [personal computers] to our staff for a token price. We also offered another incentive scheme, whereby if any of the staff or management were interested in purchasing one of the new machines, the company would subsidise 20% of the purchasing price.

The haberdashery suppliers still continue to arrange for their employees to have on-the-job demonstrations, by the appropriate specialists, whenever there is a need for new software to be introduced. The availability of experts, as trouble shooters on a need to know basis, and the presence of strong informal patterns of relationships in each section are said to be the main elements for the success of the project.

Conclusion

The social technical framework for enhancing effective transfer is an alternative to the traditional approach which tends to place the sole concern on the task- related learning processes. Transfer of training is a socio-technical phenomenon which ought to be understood and dealt with in the context of work relationships.

The significance of the socialisation processes and the extent to which they can effect behaviour for better (*facilitative* role) or for worse (*inhibitive* role) in implicit and explicit ways, in terms of the transferability of the learnt knowledge, skills, values and attitudes have been discussed. The reason for experiencing less negative transfer in cases where on-the-job training methods have been employed is argued to be mainly due to the fact that social learning processes (*socialisation*) can also take place, along with the role-related aspect of the training, simultaneously and on a routine basis.

It must be remembered that even a well designed training or re-training programme, consisting of task and people related skills, knowledge and experience may not yield the results expected. Unless it is recognised that effective transfer is a function of motivation, intrinsic and extrinsic, learning cannot effectively take place, let alone be transferred effectively to the workplace.

Of course, a socio-technical approach to the analysis of transfer, as a means for enhancing effective transfer, has its own scope and limitations. These will be dealt with in the next chapter.

6 Effective transfer and its scopes and limitations

Introduction

The proposed socio-technical approach to training and development, like any other perspective, also has its limitation for exploitation. Its potential benefits, in terms of enhancing the effective transfer of learnt material to the workplace, are determined by the presence and interaction of influential workplace social-related factors.

These factors may not necessarily be expected to be present within the classroom where training takes place or solely within the actual workplace where the act of doing is the main concern. As stated earlier, transfer ought to be regarded as a process which is initiated in the learning environment with the intention of its being extended to the job. In an on-the-job training situation the process of transfer will commence and occur in the same place - the actual workplace. In the off-the-job situation, effective transfer may include the process of both the social and technical learning, which occur at the training centre plus that learning which subsequently takes place at workplace. Thus, the process of effective transfer may involve situations and people who may not all belong to the workplace organisation.

To identify the major contributing factors involved in the extent to which socio-technical transfer can be effectively implemented, the following broad categories will be considered. These are, the learner, what is to be transferred, the trainer and the organisation. These factors are believed to constitute the main actors and components in the organisation of transfer.

The individual learner

Throughout the process, the individual learner becomes the pivotal aspect of the realisation of effective transfer. It is the individual learner who has to acquire the socio-technical knowledge, skills, values and such like in the first place, and it is the individual whose performance and behaviour at work provides the tangible evidence for measuring the extent to which transfer has taken place.

It is also important to remember that the individual, either in the position of a trainee on-the-job or as a learner in a training centre, will not only be influenced by the external environment but will also implicitly or explicitly influence the process of learning, his own and others, through his interaction with others and his participation in the learning situation.

To understand the role of the individual learner and his contribution towards the 'making or breaking' of effective transfer, the following issues need to be considered.

The individual's cognitive maps and socialisation

The case for the cognitive differences in individuals and the differences in their values and beliefs structures and their effect on behaviour, is now well recognised. The theory that the individual's behaviour is, by and large, directed by their cognitive map is one which is acknowledged by many psychologists and behavioural scientists.

Goffman, (1974) refers to the individuals unique system of values, thoughts and beliefs as 'frames of references' with which the individual perceives, interprets and understands what goes on around him. The individual's own frames of references constitutes the very foundation for the ways in which the individual's subjective map may be constructed (Broadbent, 1977). It is this which in turn provides a basis for the manner in which he conducts his social interactions (Bartlett, 1932; Neiss, 1977).

The individual's dominant schema; that is the product of one's experiences, perception of values, work roles, power dependencies, ambitions and tolerances or ambiguities, is largely responsible for his effectiveness in learning processes at both social and technical levels.

Arguably, it is these individual differences which are responsible for some learners displaying a more outstanding capacity for learning than others. This category also includes the individual's ability to act and interact with others in a social situation.

The individual's ability and preferences, when it concerns comes to socialising with others, is partly determined by his personality type which in turn determines whether the individual trainee is a 'joiner' or a 'loner'. The terms joiner and loner represent two extreme positions on the same continuum.

Both in training centres and work organisations, it has frequently been observed that people, whether in managerial or operative roles, do differ in their orientation in terms of satisfying their interpersonal (social) needs. Loners are those who are basically of an introvert nature and who tend to keep to themselves and socialise as little as possible. Joiners, however, have a greater need to become a member of a group or team and therefore prefer to accomplish tasks with others. The latter are likely to have benefited from an extrovert personality type.

The varying degrees of interpersonal needs, on the part of the individual trainees, for socialising has a determining affect in terms of their success or failure in social learning processes, the learning situation and the actual workplace. The inability on the part of the individual to interact effectively with workmates, colleagues, peers and their bosses will undoubtedly hamper the effectiveness of socialisation and may even be interpreted as an unwillingness on the part of the newcomer or returning trainee to become fully integrated into the system.

Kakabadse (1987) argues that people's 'inner directedness' and 'outer directedness' tendency based on their 'unshared' or 'shared' values, beliefs and thoughts, does influence the degree of their competence in relation to the successful outcome of their interactions with others.

The implication is that, the adoption of a socio-technical approach towards a particular training and development programme may prove difficult in situations where, for example, a trainee holds 'unshared' values and beliefs which differ from those of the dominant ideology of the learning social structure to which the individual is currently exposed. The same is also true with the learning situation which is away from the actual workplace. For example, in a management training centre it was observed that a trainee manager whose extreme political stand tended to colour most of his discussions, thus viewing all managerial situations in terms of the 'proletariat and bourgeoisie' and the exploitation of the workers by management, soon became ostracised by his fellow learners. This situation not only had a negative effect on the overall ethos of the learning situation but also resulted in the refusal, by established group members, to let him to join their syndicate work thus adopting non cooperation as a strategy to alienate him from the learning situation as a whole. The possession of values which were radically different from other trainee's added to his inability to successfully adjust to new situation and interact with the rest of the group, which meant that his technical learning also suffered considerably.

Ability to learn

While it is appropriate to assume that all individuals are capable of learning both the task and social aspects of the work for which they are being trained, it is especially correct to acknowledge that people also differ in their ability to learn, the pace at which their learning takes place (Brandura, 1977) and their preferred styles for learning. People's previous exposure to task and social learning processes, knowledge and skills in the form of education or experience will determine the amount of ease or difficulty which the learner will experience while being trained.

It was explained in Chapter Two that the concept of 'learning curve' can be used as an aid for determining the degree of positively or negatively accelerated learning of the individual learners (Glueck, 1974; James, 1984; Kennoy and Reid, 1986). Some individuals naturally tend to reach the 'plateau' (where no effective learning takes place) sooner than others. In a mixed group of learners, or employees, inevitably some will need more time and attention in order to learn and retain, for example, technical matters.

In addition, it has also been observed that the learning curve is not necessarily indicative of the progress in the social-related aspects of learning. The individual who has the aptitude and social skills for successfully interacting with others may not necessarily show the same degree of progress when it concerns the technical aspects of the job. However, observations both in industry and in training centres has revealed that the application of a socio-technical approach will be carried out with more ease if the individuals involved are sociable with an *'outer-directed'* orientation towards works and others.

Whether in a training location outside of or inside of the organisation, the individuals who can cope with the social demands of the situation will be have a better chance (or be given a longer period of grace) to learn and improve the task- related aspects of their work.

The individuals ability to learn their experience of change and their capability to cope with change, all directly affect the socio-technical learning processes. People who are open to new ideas and generally welcome change can naturally cope both physically and psychologically with the changes within the training centre and during the 'transition' period in the workplace environment.

In organisations where the 'role culture' is prevalent, people's attitude, orientation to their jobs and their concept of change is different from those who work in an environment which benefits from a 'task-culture'. It has been observed that management trainees from public sector organisations, by and large, find the process of adjustment to new ideas and coping with change as a whole, difficult and painful. In contrast, the individual trainee who had worked in a competitive work environment, has had direct experience of initiating and dealing with change situations and therefore is psychologically inclined towards uncertainty and taking risks if necessary, will perceive the process of coping with change as a challenge. Thus, in a learning situation they are more inclined to let go of the old or incompatible values and adopt new ones.

Factors such as *age* (Wellford, 1962); *commitment* (Hunt, 1979); *learning styles* (Honey & Mumford, 1982); *memory* (Haslerud 1972); *motivation* (Smith et al, 1982) and *cultural differences* (Bramley, 1990) will undoubtedly influence the extent and effectiveness of learning and its effective transfer.

Action levers

- Assist participant trainees to recognise and be aware of the presence of their own dominant value schema and action strategies.
- Enable the individual concerned to learn and become more aware of the dominant value system in operation in the social environment of the workplace (or the learning situation in case of the off-the-job training mode).
- Assist the individual trainees to identify their learning styles and preferred ways of working with the materials, values and beliefs which are to be learnt.
- Ensure that participant trainees are aware of their learning performance (positive or negative accelerated learning curve) in order that they may pace their own learning programme.
- Identify the level of the trainee's previous exposure to the technical and social aspects of the learning programme.

- Provide the opportunity for the trainee participants (in this case an off-the-job training programme) to socialise with the rest of the primary group members and thus accelerate the socialisation process.
- Avoid the formation of ill-task groups whereby one or more members of the group can not identify with the prevailing social norms of the collectivity, the task involved or both.
- Make sure that all trainee participants are aware of the individual differences in perception and of the differing value systems amongst them.

It ought to be made clear to the trainees that it is not people who differ, it is their values, thoughts and beliefs which form the basis for the presence of differences amongst them.

The trainer's role

The scope and limitation of adopting a socio-technically based training programme is largely decided by the nature of the involvement of the trainers and educators themselves, especially in an off-the-job training situation.

The role of the trainers has been the subject of many academic debates and discussions. For example, Baudhuin (1987) in his argument concerning the 'Design of Industrial and Flight Simulators', concludes that 'It may be true [...] that transfer effectiveness is more a function of how the trainer is being utilised, than the function of the simulator's fidelity' (p.234).

However, in most discussions concerning the influence of the trainer on the individual's learning the emphasis has been placed on the role of the trainer in an organisational context, thus, assessing his relationship in terms of political, social and power based, with other reference members of the immediate work setting or the workplace at large.

To mention a few, writers such as Pettigrew et al, (1982), in A Survey of Trainers in the Chemical Industry, have identified major roles, namely the 'maintainer' who provides services primarily for maintenance purposes within the organisation; the 'passive provider' who responds to demands made on him; the 'training manager' who is likely to be preoccupied with the management and establishment of training activities and the development of policies, procedure and the organisation within the enterprise; and finally, the 'change agents' who are few and far between in the main and who perceive their role as being responsible for the preparation of the organisation for change, the adoption of new policies, practices, patterns of behaviour, values and such like.

Bennett and Leduchowicz (1983) provide a novel approach for the classification of the roles that trainers usually undertake. They use the terms 'traditional' and 'interventionist' when describing the trainers' orientation and approaches towards either organisational 'maintenance' or 'change' respectively, as a basis for the identification of four major role categories. From the above 'care taker', 'educator', 'evangelist' and 'innovator' emerge as the main roles which are argued to have been adopted by trainers and practitioners within the context of organisational activities.

It must be noted that these and other classifications, as concluded by Bramley (1990) all fall between the 'traditional/reactive'and 'change agent/proactive' types.

Indeed, how trainers perceive their role and their orientation to training at large, and trainees in particular, acts as a determining factor in the process of bringing about effective transfer. The author's observations in industry and public sector organisations point to the presence of a broad two category role classification for trainers and educators.

The first, the 'maintainer' is primarily concerned with 'here and now'. Maintainers gradually develop a reactive orientation to their work and the trainees. For them the maintenance of the present standards and status quo is of prime importance. The traditional values which the maintainer holds have been shown to have become the basis for their task-related knowledge and skills. Such individuals show a preference for being in the position of 'provider' towards their trainees, and to adopt a responsive attitude towards their clients and superiors. Maintainers generally prefer to be told what to do rather than to take the initiative or to break new ground.

The director of a management training and development department of a large processing organisation, described maintainers as the type 'who make one set of overheads and use it over and over again for donkey's years'.

The second is the 'change agent', who is totally different in his approach to training, trainees and the organisation for or with which they work. He benefits from a dynamic approach to people and situations and is best characterised as proactive, one who worries about the 'future and then' rather than 'here and now'. The change agent is therefore, well aware of the historical development of the subject which he or she provides, but feels the need for the design and development of new approaches and ways of 'getting the job done'.

Experience shows that trainers, in their capacity as change agents, are least concerned with the expansion of their powerbase within the organisation, though their contribution, if they survive long enough, to the well being and progress of the organisation will become appreciated in time and is enough to provide them with an almost non-negotiable position within the organisation. The change agent, in its extreme sense, is more concerned with the people and people-related knowledge, skills and values, than the task-related aspects. He is competent in interpersonal communication and his skills, energy and enthusiasm provide him with a niche from which he can manipulate the politics of the organisation, while overtly denying the need on his part for becoming heavily involved.

The 'maintainer' and 'change agent' provide the two extremes on the identified continuum of the approaches that trainers generally adopt towards their work, the organisation and people as a whole. These roles are congruent with the task-related, people-related and socio-technical orientation to training as identified earlier in Chapter Four.

The socio-technical role represents the mid-way position between the 'maintainer' and the purely 'change agent' role extremes. This balanced position will be referred to as an 'active manager'. The active manager is one who shows more or less equal concern for, on the one hand, the maintenance of the organisation and preservation of the status quo and on the other hand acknowledges the need for adapting to or bringing about change. He sees the adoption of this twin-role attitude as necessary for the future development of the individual trainees as well as the development of the organisation as a whole.

Unfortunately, and this is probably one of the main reasons for experiencing ineffective transfer in most training situations, most trainers have shown a tendency towards being a 'maintainer' with a high concern for the task related knowledge and skills.

Here, it seems quite apt to borrow the interesting analogy used by Bennett and Oliver (1988) when discussing the dangers of believing that everyone is a good communicator and extending that to the role of trainers. 'Like sex and driving, every one believes they are good at it' (p.22). Both in industry and academia it has been frequently observed that possession of technical skills, for example, an earned Ph.D in Agricultural Tool Sharpening or Quantum Physics has often been interpreted by the holders of such impressive qualifications or indeed by the those in charge of the organisation, as proof of the individual's ability to become an effective trainer. All too often, it has been observed that such so called trainers with their mainly mechanistic attitude towards knowledge, learning, training and most important of all the trainees, fail to see their role as agents for facilitating effective training and transfer, thus remaining in their non-negotiable positions as 'providers' of 'good stuff'.

A professor with long term experience of the directorship of a prestigious training and development centre had the following experience.

> I was visiting another centre, having coffee and discussing the trend for management training amongst developing countries with the Director of the centre, when we heard a disturbance outside in his secretary's office. Apparently, she had been trying, to no avail, to stop a group of post-experience training participants from barging their way into the director's office. When Gerald enquired what the problem was, the leader of the group, a Secretary in the Presidential Office in an Eastern African country, said 'All we want is to be treated like human beings, not tape recorders and inanimate objects...'. Gerald, feeling rather embarrassed that I should have witnessed the situation, explained that it was Jeremy one of the trainers/consultants who was most enthusiastic of all and believed in a 'no nonsense' approach to management training and that 'the participants were here [in this country or in the training centre] to learn and certainly not to waste time' so he gives them few breaks and plenty to do during the weekends.... no harm in that really is there? I suppose you could say that Jeremy fits into your purely task-related model of trainers.

The reality is that, as indicated in the previous chapter, adopting a socio-technical model for training and transfer necessitates the possession of appropriate and relevant knowledge and skills on the part of the trainers involved in order to be able to deal with the people aspects of learning situations as well as its task and role-related aspects. In the case of off-the-job learning situations this is of the utmost importance if the concern is the realisation of effective transfer to the workplace environment.

Being an expert in the task-related subjects and related fields, for example, in the field of mechanical design or project management, should not be seen as a permit for claiming to adopt a socio-technical approach to training. Trainers ought to possess, not just a flair for interpersonal skills, as has been observed to be the case in most situations, but sufficient knowledge and skills for dealing with individuals, groups, developing teams, negotiating, motivating and leading the trainees towards the achievement of the prescribed task-related objectives.   As Trost (1985) aptly ascertains;

142

Trainers serve as role models and need to demonstrate the skills they are teaching. It's amazing how often communication trainers don't practice good communication skills. They cut off participants questions, move on to other topics before the group is ready and fail to use listening [an interpersonal skill] responses (p.79).

In situations where the complexity of the task involved, the learning of new knowledge, skills, values and attitudes - in the case of managerial training - or the lack of suitable trainers or learning environments compels employers to choose outside methods of training, the importance of the socio-technical competences on the part of the trainers in the training centre chosen gains even more importance.

It is envisaged that an inability to create a conducive facilitating learning environment on the part of the trainers involved undoubtedly leads to ineffective learning. Once the trainees, with little or inappropriately acquired amounts of learnt task-related knowledge and skills have been physically transferred to the actual workplace, no amount of positive socialisation and motivation in the workplace will result in the occurrence of the transfer of knowledge and skills which had not been effectively learnt in the first instance.

It seems therefore, inappropriate to blame the off-the-job methods of training for the lack of transfer, when in reality the reasons for ineffective transfer could chiefly be laid within the trainers own wrong attitudes and their purely task-related approach to training and their trainees as a whole.

Action levers

- Make trainers and educators aware of the importance of the socio-technical principles to effective learning, training and transfer.
- Assist trainers to identify their personal level of need and understanding of the people-related knowledge, information and 'know how' skills in subject areas, such as perception, communication, motivation, leadership and the like.
- Enable trainers to design course content in such a way that ample opportunity is provided for supervised and unstructured 'primary socialisation' amongst the group members.
- Promote and reward the participatory styles of training amongst the trainers, in order to facilitate the learning processes both at the social and technical levels whilst trainees are at the centre.
- Ensure that provision is made for trainees to become aware of the

socialisation and transition processes which they will encounter when they re-enter their actual workplace. Trainers have to understand the process of coping with change and empower their trainees to deal with this inevitable experience when returning to work.

- Ensure that trainers are familiar with the various 'operating cultures' in the public and private sectors in which trainees work and that they are generally aware of the cultural differences and their effect on learning amongst their participants, should they culturally constitute a non homogeneous group.

- Where the cultural differences amongst the trainee participants are so great that they cannot be bridged easily, self-directed learning should be used, either as a last resort or as a supplementary learning method, to ensure that adequate learning has taken place. Trainers have to learn to manage learning and training situations in a participative and democratic manner, in order to ensure that the socio-technical approach to transfer works.

- Trainers should become aware of the importance of evaluating and assessing the training programme, based on the socio-technically learnt and acquired knowledge and skills.

In the same way that the trainees require support and supervision, the educators and trainers also need organisational and managerial support in order to remain effective. This should include provision of opportunities for their professional development. Zanger (1985), the President of Zanger-Miller Inc, who has been involved in training and development projects for many organisations argues that, managerial support for trainers is short of what is expected and is never properly defined.

> Fundamentally, we have discovered that many training groups fail to receive total support because they never really ask for it in specific, precise terms. They ask for 'support' and are told that the training function has management's 'support'. The problem is that support is never defined, and while upper management truly believes they are giving it, the training functions believe they are receiving very little (p.4).

If trainers, by acting as though they are 'managers', are expected to show the way to others and to prepare operatives and managers to be able to achieve the prescribed goals of the organisation, then in the first instance the trainers themselves ought to be enabled to deliver the 'goods' and to learn how to manage the training functions. In an in-house training situation, it is relatively easier for the trainers to adopt the socio-technical principles, than it is for their colleagues who work in training centres which are away from client organisations. Yet both groups, particularly the latter, still require training and development in order to remain effective. What ought to be avoided at all costs, is the situation where 'the blind is asked to lead the blind'.

The organisation: the boss

The most crucial aspect of the process of effective transfer, in a socio-technical context, was identified as being the workplace itself. In Chapter Four, the importance of a smooth experience of transition, the role of the organisation and of the boss in ensuring the success of this critical stage was discussed in detail. It was demonstrated how, especially in the case of on-the-job training, the support that the organisation renders to the trainers and trainees, accelerates the process of integration and leads to an increased effectiveness of the transfer.

The further away the training situation is from the actual workplace, the more problematic the process of effective socialisation is within the workplace. Therefore, the application of a socio-technical framework to increase the effectiveness of the transfer, has to be carried out in stages.

First, at the learning centre, when the trainee is a member of an small primary group. In this artificial social learning situation usually the trainer replaces the 'boss' for the employee and guides the trainee in his journey of learning and acquiring various skills.

The second stage of learning occurs in the actual organisation itself. The boss or immediate superior, line manager and even executives with whom the individual trainee works, will have to act as an informal trainer and role model for the employee. Of course, there is a myriad of factors in any organisation which affects the nature and effectiveness of the transfer, from which the boss or immediate superior constitute only one, albeit an important one. The organisation's policies and procedures for the selection, recruitment and training and development of employees, as well as appraisal and development, the nature of the work to be carried out, the size and location of the workplace, its history and the overall ethos of the social system all play decisive roles towards 'facilitating' or 'inhibiting' the transfer from taking place.

The immediate boss, his attitude and managerial style towards work and people remains the most single important factor which not only affects the employee's learning or relearning but also affects the process of converting the learnt material, skills and knowledge into practice. Managers who adopt an authoritarian leadership style, tend to perceive the accomplishment of task as the only reason for which the individual is being employed by the organisation. Thus, inevitably, an early period of ineffectiveness which is usually experienced by the trainees in their initial stage of transition, is either regarded as 'defiance' or interpreted as reduced learning potential on the part of the learner. The trainee's performance is only assessed in terms of their ability to do the job (role) which should preferably result in a quantifiable output and not necessarily in terms of their ability and willingness to successfully socialise into the social system and become familiar with the cultural aspects of the workplace.

At the other extreme, some managers have been observed to adopt a purely people-related style which neglects the task-related issues and activities. The trainee involved, may feel that 'no one is really interested in his performance'.

The successful application of a socio-technical framework requires the creation of a dynamic and two way interaction between the boss and the trainee to ensure that as the trainee goes through the learning processes and his needs and expectations change, the manager is able to recognise and identify these needs and can begin to adopt a complimentary attitude towards the individual. The support which is given to the individual in the form of consultation, advice and even supervision and monitoring of his work, should gradually be reduced and replaced with additional responsibility and opportunities for the trainee concerned to effectively put the learnt material, knowledge and skills into practice. The 'manager controlled learning' attitude and style should gradually be replaced by the 'trainee controlled doing' as the learning progresses.

Indeed, the scope and limitation of adopting socio-technical principles for the realisation of effective transfer is mainly decided by whether the organisation and bosses concerned firmly believe in the policy of 'sink or swim' for their new or retrained employees or whether they believe in the value of assisting and preparing their employees to 'learn and survive' the formal and informal social assault course of the workplace. It is necessary for practitioners to possess or acquire the knowledge and skills which are needed to correctly identify the trainees degree of need for 'recognition', 'affiliation' and exercising 'control' over their jobs. Understanding trainees socio-technical and interpersonal needs and acting upon them promptly is essential for the success of a training programme.

146

Despite the differences in the methods of training used, eventually and indeed inevitably the trainees have to return to their respective jobs, where their performance in the actual workplace will be subjected to the informal assessment, evaluation and appraisal of their colleagues, peers and superiors.

In either on or off-the-job training situations, whether the programme is designed to benefit operatives or management trainees, or whether the training concerns learning simple or complex knowledge or skills, values and attitudes, all these learning processes, social or technical, ought to be contracted between the trainer and trainee and the trained and the boss concerned. A learning contract between a boss and an operative could include the use of mutually agreed upon performance and learning charts, on which the individual trainee and the manager both register their observations. Transfer-related meetings must be held on a regular basis so that the problems and difficulties experienced by the trainees are discussed and joint solutions for their resolution are made.

In the case of off-the-job training situations, transfer should not be expected to occur within the first few days of the individual's return to his post. A programme for the realisation of what is regarded by both the individual and his manager as a fair and realistic measure for the occurrence of transfer should jointly be devised, agreed upon and implemented. The limitation or scope of the application of a socio-technical framework for the effective transfer of training is, by and large, determined by how committed the organisation and its managers are to systematically initiating, facilitating and accelerating the process of the recovery of their employees' learnt knowledge and acquired skills and its transformation into sustainable performance.

Action lever

- Ensure that trainees are aware of the nature and demands of the learning processes in which they will be involved.
- Make sure the fundamantal difference between 'learning' and 'doing' is understood, and that the degree of improved performance is seen as a combination of both technical and social competence.
- Provide the trained or trainees with a socio-technically aware supervisor [not just any Nelly] to closely work with.
- Monitor the progress of the individuals' role-related performance and their social learning processes regularly.

- Involve both the learners and their supervisor in your periodical transfer-related meetings to set mutually agreed objectives. Establish realistic measures by which the attainment of agreed objectives can be monitored.
- Assist the individual and his supervisor (probationers) to identify the potential organisationally based *inhibitors* and *facilitators* which may affect the learning or the performance of the trainee concerned.
- Encourage the trainees to adopt their own preferred style, programme and policies for effective socialisation and improved task performance.
- Provide the trainee with ample opportunities for trying out newly acquired skills, knowledge and values.
- Allow for periods of low productivity during the course of *transition* and be prompt in providing the necessary motivation and support to see trainees through the 'relearning' stage of the transition process.
- Move away from the 'dependency' stage towards 'autonomy' and 'self-directed' learning, on a gradual and planned basis and encourage the trainee to gain control over the process of *learning* and *doing* in the organisation.
- Wean the individual off the primary support, but do not cut off completely the provision of support and encouragement to him.
- Encourage the individual to display, use and integrate their acquired knowledge, skills and values into their work.

Conclusion

The extent of the effectiveness of this approach to effective training, development and transfer is largely determined by how it is used and with what degree of conviction it is implimented. The socio-technical approach to the transfer of training should be regarded as one whole process whose major stages, for example, learning in or outside of the organisation, its actors, trainees, trainers, managers and other reference individuals, all act and interact with one another thus effecting the outcome and the degree of effective transfer.

It is virtually impossible to make effective transfer happen, for example in a situation where the individual has not acquired the role-related aspects of the job, in the first place; or the trainer is familiar with the concept and but has not been equipped with the people-related skills necessary for its implementation; or it may be the case that the organisation is not receptive to the social and technical requirements of the individual for effectively performing the job.

Each stage of effective transfer is intricately related to the next and committment on the part of the individual, the trainers, the organisation and its managers is necessary and essential for the completion of the process. A closed system approach to the organisation of training which limits the control which the individual learner, has over their own learning processes, views the trainers as only 'providers' and 'maintainers' and which does not set out to create an effective social environment at work, is bound to experience ineffective transfer. Organisations with management who are not sensitive to the training and development needs of their employees and trainers and only seek to get the job done as cheaply and as quickly as possible, can not benefit from the socio-technical approach to training and transfer. The philosophy and principles of the socio-technical approach to training and transfer, nevertheless can be learnt and mastered by those who intend to adopt it.

More than just willingness, on the part of the trainees and trainers is required to ensure the realisation of the effective transfer. For one thing, the prevailing value structure (culture) of the workplace should be made amenable to the idea of self-learning and to assisting employees to learn, as a routine aspect of the organisational activities and life.

It is widely acknowledged that the individual's values structure and to a large extent the organisational culture are influenced, if not shaped, by the powerful structural factors such as legal, political, socio-economic and cultural issues, which are present and operating within the context of the wider society. The presence of these factors, the degree and extent of their impact on the training programme and the eventual transfer of that programme ought to be recognised and their role as inhibitors and facilitators for the transfer of learning should be taken into consideration.

Thus, in a way the parameters for the effectiveness of the socio-technical approach are determined by the utilising organisations, their training and development policies and the extent to which trainers and educators wish to include the above external and organisational factors. Components such as the availability of resources, supervision before, during and after the termination of training, the design, structure and content of a training programme, and the trainers' style of managing learning situations as opposed to maintaining them, are the main determinants of the scope and limitations of this approach to training.

7 The future of transfer

Introduction

In discussing the problem of transfer, in the context of learning and more specifically in the context of training, it has been attempted to view the issue from a different perspective than those which have been adopted by contemporary psychologists who are primarily concerned with cognition and individual differences, theorists preoccupied with learning and recollecting and a whole host of writers generally interested in worthwhile training. To achieve this objective, the concept of the transfer of learning has been tackled in the following order.

A summary .....

First, the well-known traditional views and assumptions concerning training and the significance of transfer for the realisation of effective training have been considered. Then came debate and discussions of the major learning processes and their relevance for industrial training activities; the relevance of the methods used and their potential for effective transfer; the actual workplace and the 'socialisation' processes; the construction of a socio-technical model for the analysis of transfer and

150

finally, the analysis of the scope and limitations of adopting a socio-technical approach in order to initiate and enhance effective transfer.

In the discussion of the traditional views and beliefs about training, as a whole, and the issue of transfer in particular, it was demonstrated that contemporary writers and training specialists treatment of the subject has largely been based on mechanical conceptions supported by the kind of philosophy, principles and beliefs which have been immensely influenced, if not wholly determined by, the presuppositions derived from positivism. Training, has often been viewed in the form of a cycle whose constituent activities typically begin with the identification of training needs, appraising the alternatives available and arriving at a decision often in view of the cost involved, implementation of the intended activities and finally and typically, evaluating the result.

Traditionally in the related literature discussion concerning the issue of transfer is rarely included in the proposed cyclical model. The topic of transfer, which is habitually referred to in the context of learning and not necessarily in association with training, has been dealt with either as an appendage to the discussion of learning and learning principles or has been dealt with where the 'fidelity' of the training device has been technically discussed. Either way, transfer has largely remained in isolation from the training, training centres, the individual trainee, the learning processes involved and the dynamics of the actual workplace where in reality the results of the training are expected to be shown.

The confusion as well as concern over the issue of transfer has been highlighted when the contemporary explanations, thoughts and views which are held about the subject were discussed. More importantly the inadequate ways in which transfer has been dealt with have been analysed not merely in order to criticise the content but in order to understand the authors' beliefs, underlying assumptions, and their formation. The reader has been guided so that he may see for himself the analytical shortcomings and deficiencies present in the theory, and practice associated with transfer. By directing his attention to the crucial point that *transfer* has nearly always been traditionally seen as being associated with and relevant to 'learning', but not necessarily to training. The reason for this, as one would naturally suspect, is because in any given training situation *learning* of one form or another has to initially take place before any *doing* can be expected.

In the early stages of our discussion, the emphasis was deliberately placed on highlighting the need, on the part of researchers, trainers and specialists, to distinguish between *learning* and *doing*. Training is about learning to 'do' something and not necessarily learning for the sake of having learnt something without the need to incorporate its effects into a desired action. The evaluation test and inquiries generally are not designed primarily to assess the degree of positive transfer but are mainly focussed on how much the learner has retained, can recite or can remember of what he had been exposed to in the learning situation. Not surprisingly, the outcome of these elaborate activities is usually nothing but the measurement of the learning which has taken place and not necessarily the influence and/or impact which that learning will have on the performance and behaviour of the individual when in the workplace.

On completion of a training programme an evaluation is carried out with the intention of establishing how effective the course or programme has been for the participants involved. Such attempts, in reality, can only go as far as to measure and determine the extent to which the material, ideas, values and attitudes have transferred to the learners' short and long term memory. What they cannot do, as stated earlier, is to establish the amount of transfer in terms of 'improved performance'.

The very fact that most trainers and educators, in professional schools and training centres, have been delightedly and jubilantly celebrating the end of a another training course, when there is no concrete indication what so ever that the learning which has taken place will be transferred to the actual workplace, is itself an indication of how short sightedly the issue of transfer has traditionally been dealt with. It was for this reason that in the early part of the discussions, before moving on to learning principles and training and transfer, that the need for the consideration of the concept of transfer in its entirety, preferably in context of training was much emphasised.

The case of the organ transplant patient, which was employed as an analogy to represent the knowledge and skills newly acquired through training, was also used to show the special need for adopting an open system approach, at least towards the analysis and understanding of the multi-faceted transfer. Transfer, therefore, has been regarded not as an isolated stage but as a process which begins with learning, either in an on-the-job or off-the-job situation and terminates when the individual arrives in the actual workplace. It includes the learner, the trainer, the methods used, their attitudes and approaches, and above all the individual and the whole socialisation process which takes place in the actual workplace.

A distinction, therefore, has been made between the orthodox approach which is characterised by its technical or purely task-related views and the treatment of transfer and the reality of the actual situation in which transfer is expected to occur - the organisation. The reality of work organisations, is believed to be of an 'interpretative nature' open to negotiation at all levels by all involved parties. Therefore, it can only be adequately explained by the references made to its dynamic socio-technical properties in which learning continually takes place and is hopefully transferred in terms of improved or desired performance.

The reader is recommended to avoid at all costs the rigid law like analysis of transfer which advocates a rigidity of learning principles, of the individual's capacity for learning, relearning and retaining what is learnt and of the styles of teaching and its expected outcome as though people are nothing but memory banks or robots - a kind of explanation which incidentally has failed over and over again to adequately explain transfer.

Of course, learning and training are not one and the same thing but are closely related and the nature of their interdependency is complex. The point is, however, that in treating transfer from a socio-technical perspective rather than from a purely role-related and mechanical stand, the social learning processes which largely decide the degree of effective acquisition of knowledge and skills and then their transfer to the job, has been treated as an integral part of the process of transfer. It is, therefore, advocated here that, firstly, learning ought to be carried out in such a way that it does not place the learner in the passive position of being completely 'controlled' which increases the chances that negative transfer will occur when the learning course or programme is terminated. Instead, it is demonstrated that as views concerning people and their potential for learning and doing have changed over the years, so has their perception about their preferred ways of learning and acquiring knowledge and skills. Perhaps we should ask, is there a need for moving away from the employment of traditional learning methods and teaching and move towards viewing transfer in a different light?

In order to maintain a high degree of realism in dealing with the intricate and ever complex phenomenon of transfer, not only have the major theoretical developmental stages of learning theories and the underlying assumptions concerning learning and learners been reviewed here but also the analysis has been extended to include the trainers and practitioners who have contributed to the present low transfer of learnt material to the workplace. Discussions concerning the psychological development of the subject, includes advice and guidance for the non specialist trainer, have been provided with the aim of achieving higher rates of effective transfer partly through improving the early stages of transfer - the learning.

When the question, *do training methods integrate or separate the learner from the actual work environment?* was originally posed, the intention had been to highlight the importance of the perceived relationship between the effectiveness of the training methods, by which learning is initiated and ensured and the degree of expected effective training which is measured in terms of transferred learnt material and skills. Fortunately, it has been understood and recognised even by the traditionalists that as the complexity of the material, skills and values to be learnt increases, the choice that training should be carried out within the actual workplace decreases and therefore quite naturally, though it is still not regarded as an obvious point to many, the effectiveness of transfer also begins to suffer.

While exploring the differences present amongst the methods utilised by trainers within industry for training operatives and managerial staff, it was argued that there seems to be a plausible relationship between effective transfer and that of the proximity of the location of the learning situation to the actual workplace.

The fact that the nature of the training method to which a trainee is subjected and the method by which the training institution hopes to achieve its objectives are inherently related, itself highlights the crucial importance of the most obvious, yet much neglected phenomena directly related to the concept of transfer. That is, the influence of the learning of the dominant workplace related social value system (socialisation) and its impact on the degree of transferability of the material and skills learnt elsewhere, perhaps outside of the organisation in a training centre.

The training literature, by and large, appears to place substantial emphasis on the trainee's need to *do* a job satisfactorily and consequently focuses on the technical requirement of the job. This is often carried out quite effectively but at the expense of the social (organisational) needs of the trainees and their competence in successfully interacting with other members of their primary social community in that particular training programme.

A phrase which is popular amongst trainers and specialists, 'filling the gap' between the present performance and the desired performance, is more evidence in support of the argument that whenever performance is considered it is usually seen in terms of its role-related properties and content rather than in terms of its inherent demands for social interactions with others.

One implication of this kind of diagnostic and prognostic approach to training and consequently to its transfer is the emergence of the inevitable misconception that a training programme starts with inexperienced trainees (or less experienced) and must end with a considerable amount of change in either their performance or their behaviour, or both. The whole training affair, from the very beginning of the 'needs analysis' to the 'construction' and 'evaluation' stage is dealt with in such a way that there appears to be a conspiracy to exclude the vital socialisation processes and their impact on learning and transfer.

The adoption of a mechanistic approach to training, by traditionalists, has meant that the analysis of the current processes and contemporary methods by which people are socialised in the workplace has been deliberately under estimated. It is therefore, not surprising to see that such a low level of transfer has been experienced when off-the-job training methods have been employed as a means for filling the performance related gap. As Candy (1991), in his most valuable contribution to date on the subject of 'self-directed learning', advocates and which has significant implications for our debate concerning transfer, 'the [trainers'] underlying assumptions concerning the learning, the required learning skills, the learners capacity and the reasons for such learning, needs to be questioned so that the importance of the ways in which the trainees have been treated is understood'.

Trainers and educators have had to come to terms with the realities of training and transfer as it is (low) and not as it should be. Learners or as in our case, trainees have been observed to and have reported confidentially that on arrival at the actual workplace they have had to consciously and deliberately begin a process of self initiated unlearning in order to cope with the organisational expectations and to meet the demands made upon them by their colleagues, peers and superiors

The prevailing assumption that 'people should do as they are taught or told, or both', which is characteristically shared by those who ascribe to the orthodox and scientific approach to learning and training, is no longer acceptable in the real world of work organisations of the 90's. People make conscious decisions as to how they should behave and why. A new direction to realise effective transfer also, amongst other things, includes consideration of the voluntary nature of human beings, as actors who act and interact with others within the organisational and wider socio-economic context.

....and concluding remarks

It is concluded, therefore, that since the organisation plays such a significant role, both in terms of determining the effectiveness of the method to be adopted (proximity to the job) in terms of being the place in which the new or modified behaviours must finally be displayed, it is of the utmost importance to consider the socio-psychological climate of the workplace into which the trained or retrained individual is to enter (or re-enter) after training.

Training is about change and its transfer will inevitably include the psychological process of coping with change - the process of transition. It is understandable how the mechanistic orientation towards the comprehension of the issue of training, coupled with the impact of the orthodox presuppositions concerning the issue of knowledge (as concrete and hard) and the model of Man (as passive and only responsive to knowledge) has lead to the presence of an over optimistic attitude, the misconception that as long as the material to be learnt is properly chosen (by the trainer and not in consultation with the trainee or his organisation), and that the necessary motivation is utilised (of a *seductive* or *coersive* nature), the maximum amount of transfer will automatically follow.

Further, in a training situation, so long as situations remain stable the prevailing tendency is to use the negative feedback system to correct the course of events. In doing so, it is thought that problems only exist at the beginning of the programme and not in the workplace, where the results of the training are expected to materialise. The learner is blamed for not being able to take advantage of the learning and training opportunity and his competence and ability to retain or put into practice what has been learnt is questioned.

The trainers on the other hand, from their ivory towers, blame the trainees and the management of traditional training and learning situations, and advocate that more training and resources should be allocated and made available to off-the-job training. This attitude, by and large, ignores the possibility that the social psychological climate of the organisation and the dynamic processes involved in the social structure of the workplace can and do have influence on the degree of effectiveness of a training programme and consequently on the amount of transfer which occurs.

In practical terms, the introduction of a socio-technical perspective in the analysis, design and implementation of a training programme is believed to provide a sensible and realistic approach towards the enhancement of our present understanding of 'transfer' and also to provide practical solutions to its problems.

Thus, in constructing a socio-technical model for the analysis of the transfer of training, it has been emphasised that an improved level of transfer of learning can be realistically achieved in almost any training situation, simply by regarding any training activity as consisting of the attainment of highly distinguishable and interrelated sets of objectives.

First, the technical requirement (technical aspects of the job) which has already been generously and to a certain extent disproportionately represented in the available literature.

Secondly, the inclusion of the socialisation (social aspects of the job) to which any individual trainee will be subjected; and

Thirdly, the social learning processes which are involved in any training situation, both at the primary level within the learning situation away from the actual work environment and those which inevitably occur within the workplace, act as facilitators or inhibitors (depending on the degree of their compatibility with the needs and requirements of the situation) towards the positive and effective occurrence of transfer.

The traditional approach to training - with a disproportionate amount of stress placed on the 'technical' aspects of a training programme such as need analysis, planning, appraisal, implementation and finally the evaluation of the programme - must be considered in conjunction with the requirements of the individual trainees and the organisation concerned for 'social' learning at the different stages of training. For instance, if it is intended that a training programme should achieve its professed objective, which is filling the gap between the present and the desired levels of performance, the same degree of attention which is given to the role-related aspect of the job should also be given to the socio-psychological needs of the trainees. Relevant activities which are aimed at facilitating the learning of the people-related knowledge, skills, attitudes and values must, therefore, be included in the design of the training programme, in order that the identified 'social performance gap' is decreased.

It has also been recommended that a distinction must be made between the interrelated but separate issues of effective learning and effective transfer. An effective training programme will then be the aggregate result of the interaction between the former and the latter processes.

The application of a solely technical approach to training and transfer implies that the people involved in a learning activity should be regarded as functioning in a similar fashion to mechanical devices with a predetermined capacity for learning, retaining and conveying the learnt material to the work environment. From this purely psychological point of view, people seem to have been equated with, at best, as clever 'rats' who's responses can be conditioned to ensure that they will perform as they are instructed. In contrast with this tradition, it has been suggested here that trainees must be regarded as potentially political actors who join an organisation or a training programme primarily to enhance their own personal objectives, such as furthering their knowledge and skills, having a weekend off, a chance to gain future promotion, the possibility of an increase in power base or attaining decision making status.

In dealing with effective transfer, it is recommended that a new taxonomy ought to be used which considers the effectiveness of transfer and the need for its improvement in the context of the organisation and the kind job for which an individual is being trained. The conditions for achieving and maintaining effective transfer will be largely determined, not just by the mode of training used and their proximity to the work environment, but also by the issue of whether or not after the completion of the training programme the individual would be entering a new job, going back to a known job but in a new workplace or to a new job in an old work setting .

Considerable stress has been placed on the socialisation processes and how we must ensure that the issue of social learning processes is taken seriously. The contemporary writers on training do emphasise on the need for designing and constructing a learning situation which is close to the reality of the actual workplace. The most intriguing point about this assumption is that the 'reality of the situation' in the organisation is only considered in its physical sense, such as ensuring the presence of the similarity between the stimuli and response, the physical arrangement and layout of the equipment and machinery, but the need for incorporating the 'social realities' into the training is seldom considered to be a worth while activity.

The potential and limitations of a socio-technical approach to training and transfer is largely determined by human factors including the trainees themselves, the instructors and educators, managers, colleagues and even the clients of the organisation. Whilst it is hoped that the guide-lines and action levers provided will be of benefit to the trainers, instructors and practitioners in industry and training centres, the fact that the ultimate responsibility for the realisation of effective transfer can not be placed on the trainee, trainer or even the manager alone needs to be reiterated.

The first hand experience of on-the-job training programmes in industry, the observations made in training institutions, and the contemporary political, social and economical trends all point to the continued presence of training in the future as a means towards improving performance, productivity and development at an individual, institutional and industrial level. Training will never become 'old hat' so long as organisations have to ensure that the Peter Principle does not occur on their door step.

Traditionally, the reasons for alleged incompetence and ineffectiveness on the part of operatives and managers are seen as being mainly due to the inability of the role holders to get the job done as specified. While training provides a promising avenue towards achieving the organisation goal, the lack of effective or even negative transfer can simply be interpreted as a deliberate misuse of financial resources at organisational level and waste of human capacity and resources on a grand scale. Effective transfer can be achieved if the processes that influence and determine its effective occurrence are understood and hence incorporated into the design and implementation of a training programme. The problem of transfer, therefore, ought to be viewed from a much broader perspective than it traditionally has been. This necessitates a change of attitudes on the part of theorists, trainers and educators and most important of all the employers towards people, learning, training, transfer and the organisation as the whole. Also to consider the crucial issue of the reality of the organisation in its entirety towards the development of its employees and their effectiveness and efficiency as a whole.

Training as an organisational activity and the means for initiating and sustaining change, as far as possible, ought to be incorporated into the work processes. Training should not be considered as an isolated activity which has to await the termination of the programme before concern for its transfer is felt necessary.

Adopting an Action Learning approach, to both learning and effective training will undoubtedly lead the way towards ensuring the effectiveness of training and its possible transfer. This requires viewing organisations in a different light - as real learning environments and as an appropriate context for bringing about the necessary change in individuals, groups performance, their values, and work related attitudes. Effective learning, should be viewed as a life long concern, for both operatives and managers. Self-directedness and commitment on the part of the employees and support from their peers, colleagues and superiors need to form the prerequisites and basic foundation towards realising effective transfer.

Adhering to the socio-technical perspective principles for understanding transfer requires the ability and willingness to change, on the part of the learners, trainers and those in charge of work organisations. These actors ought to accept that the realities of work and work organisations are about 'uncertainties' and complex socio-psychological processes which do not necessarily support the traditional views concerning learning and working in an orderly and predetermined world.

In the real world of the contemporary work organisations which is characterised by the need for constant change and the ability on the part of its human constituents to effectively cope with contradictions and ambiguity in every aspect of its activities, transfer can not be regarded only as an aspect of learning or even training, rather it ought to be considered as an aspect of organisational reality. Organisations with their varying social and task-related cultures, their specific and implied objectives and their varied activities represent a milestone in the need for understanding the complex process of realising effective transfer which, as shown here, can only be adequately understood within its socio-technical context.

Bibliography

Adams, J. A. (1968), 'Response feedback and learning', *Psychological Bulletin*, no. 70.

Adams, B., Hayes, J. & Hopson, B. (1976), *Transitio Understanding and Managing Personal Change*, Martin Roslestson.

Adomaitis, A. (1984), 'Investigation into Low Success rates of Slimming Clubs', Unpublished Masters Thesis, University of Lancaster.

Alderfer, C. P. (1972), *Existence, Relatedness, and Growth: Human Needs in Organisational Setting*, Free Press, London.

Analoui, F. (1989) 'Social Organisation of Transfer of Learning: An Exploration of a neglected aspect of training and development' *Occasional Paper* No. 14, Development and Project Planning Centre, University of Bradford

Analoui, F. (1990),'Training and Effective Transfer: a socio - technical approach', *Project Appraisal*, Vol. 5, no. 3, PP 175 -179.

Annett, J. (1961), The Role of the Knowledge of Result in Learning: A Survey, *US Naval Training Devices Centre*. Vol. 31, no. 23, pp 342-3.

Annett, J. (1969), *Feedback and Human Behaviour,* Penguin, Harmondsworth, UK.

Annett, J. (1983), Skill Loss, in Kenney, J. and Reid, M. (1986), *Training Intervention*, Institute of Personnel Management, London.

Argyris, C. (1964), *Integrating the Individual and the Organisation*, John Wiley & Sons, Inc., New York.

Attneave, F. (1959), *Application of Information Theory toPsychology,* Holts, Rinehart and Winston, New York.

Bartlett, S.F. (1932) *Remembering*, Cambridge University Press, Cambridge.

Bass, B. M. and Vaughan, J. A. (1966), *Training in Industry - the management of learning*, Tavistock Publication, London.

Baudhuin, E.S. (1987) 'The Design of Industrial and Flight Simulators' in Cormier, S. M., Hagman, S.D. *Training and Transfer: Contemporary Research and Application*, Academic Press Inc, New York.

Beach, D. (1980), *Personnel: The Management of People at Work*, Macmillan Publication Co, New York.

Bennett, R. (1988), *Improving Training Effectiveness*, Gower, Aldershot, England.

Bennett, R. & Leduchowicz, T. (1983), 'What makes for an effective trainer?' *Journal of European Industrial Training Monograph*, Vol. 7, No. 2, MCB Publication.

Bennett, R. & Oliver, J. (1988), How to Get the Best from Action Research - A Guidebook, *Journal of Leadership and Organisational Development*, Vol. 9, No. 3, MCB University Press.

Berne, E. (1961), *Transactional Analysis in Psychotherapy*, Grove Press, New York.

Blumfield, W. S. & Holland, M. G. (1971), 'A Model for Empirical Evaluation of Training Effectiveness', *Personnel Journal*, Vol. 1, no. 50, August.

Bramley, P. (1990), *Evaluating Training Effectiveness: Translating Theory into Practice*, McGraw-Hill Training Series, London.

Brandura, A. (1977), *Learning Theory*, Prentice Hall, New York.

Breakwell, G. M. & Gilmour, R. (1982), *Socio-Psychology - A Practical Manual*, British Psychological Society and Macmillan Press Ltd.

Broadbent, D. E. (1977), Hidden Pre-Active Processes, *American Psychologist*, Vol. 32, No. 1.

Brown, J.A.C. (1965), *The Social Psychology of Industry* (5th Edition) Penguin Books, Harmondsworth, London

Burrel, G. & Morgan, G. (1979), *Sociological Paradigms and Organisational Analysis*, Heinemann, London.

Campbell, J. (1970), *Managerial Behaviour*, McGraw-Hill Book Co., New York.

Candy, P. C. (1991), *Self-Directed Learning For Lifelong Learning*, Jossey-Bass Limited, San Francisco.

Casio, W.F. (1982), *Costing Human Resources; The Financial Impact of Behaviour in Organisations*. Kent, Boston.

Copeman, S. (1951), *Leaders in British Industry*, Gee & Co., London.

Cormier, S. M. & Hagman, D. J. (1987), *Transfer of Learning: Contemporary Research and Applications*, (Ed), Academic Press INC., London.

Davies, I. K. (1971), *Management Of Learning,* McGraw Hill Books Co. (UK), London.

Davies, I. K. (1973), *The Organisation of Training*, (Ed), McGraw Hill Books Co. (UK), London.

Department of Employment (1971), *Glossary of Training Terms*, (2nd ed), H.M.S.O., London.

Duncan, K. D. & Kelly, C. J. (1983), *Task Analysis, Learning and the Nature of Transfer*, Manpower Services Commission, Sheffield.

Ellis, H. C. (1965), *The transfer of learning*, Macmillan, New York.

Ellis, S. K. (1989), *How to survive a training assignment*, Addison-Wesley.

English, H. B. & English, A. C. (1958), *A Comprehensive Dictionary of Psychological and Psycho-analytical Terms*, Longman Green & Co., New York.

Fleishman, E. A. (1953), 'Leadership Climate, Human Relation Training and Supervisory Behaviour', *Personnel Psychology*, Vol. 1, no. 6, pp. 205-20.

Gagne, R. M. (1970), *The Conditions of Learning*, 2nd ed, Holt Rinehart and Winston, New York.

Glueck, W. F. (1974), *Personnel: A Diagnostic Approach*, Irwin-Dorsey International, London.

Goffman, I. (1977), *Frame Analysis: An Essay on the Organisation of Experience*. Penguin, London.

Golembueski, R. T. (1976), *Learning and Change in Groups*, Penguin Modern Psychology, London.

Gross, R. D. (1991), *Psychology - The Science of Mind and Behaviour*, Hodder & Stoughton, London.

Handy, C. (1985), *Understanding Organisations*, Penguin Books, England.

Harlow, H. F. (1949), 'Formation of learning set', *Psychological Review*, no. 56, PP. 51-65.

Haslerud, G. (1972), *Transfer, Memory and Creativity*, University Press, London.

Hayes, J. (1990), 'Perceptions of the Factors Which Influence the Transfer of Learning: An Indian Case Study', *Journal of Public Sector Management*, Vol. 3, no. 1.

Hazes, C., Fonda, N., Pope, N., Stuart, R & Townsend, K. (1983), *Training For Skill Ownership*, Brighton Institute of Manpower Studies.

Hertzberg, F. (1968), *Work and the Nature of Man*, Staples Press, London.

Hertzberg, F.(1968), 'One More Time: How Do You Motivate Your Employees?', *Harvard Business Review*, Vol. 46, pp 53-62.

Hertzberg, F., Mausner, B., & Snyderman, B. (1959), *The Motivation to Work*, Wiley, New York.

Hinrichs, J. R. (1976), 'Personnel Training', in Dunnette,M.D.(ed.), *Handbook of Organisational and Industrial Psychology*, Rand McNally, Chicago.

Holding, D. H. (1965), *Principles of Learning*, Pergamon Press, Oxford.

Holloway, C. (1974),'Organisation feedback and goal-directed behaviour', *Human Information Processing*, (part 1), Open University Press, Keegan Page, London.

Honey, P. & Mumford, A. (1982), *The Manual of Learning Styles*, Honey, Berkshire, England.

Hunt, J. (1981), *Managing People at Work*, Pan Books Ltd, London.

Hyman, R. (1972), *Strikes*, Fontana-Collins, London.

Jackson, K. F. (1948), *The Art of Solving Problems*, Bulmershe-Comino Problem Solving Project, Reading College of Higher Education.

James, R. (1984), 'The Use of Learning Curves' *Journal of European Industrial Training*. Vol, 8, No. 7.

Jones, M. (1979), 'Training Practices and Learning Theories', *Journal of European Industrial Training*, Vol. 3, no. 7, March.

Kakabadse, A. (1987), *Working in Organisations*, Gower, University Press, Cambridge.

Kakabadse, A & Mukhi, S. (eds) (1984), *The Future of Management Education*, Gower Nichols Publishing, New York.

Katz, D. & Kahn, R. (1966), *The Social Psychology of Organisations*, John Wiley & Sons, New York.

Katz, D. & Kahn, R. (1978), *Social Psychology of Organisations*, 2nd Ed. John Wiley & Sons, London.

Kay, H. (1983), 'Accidents: some facts and theories', in *Psychology at Work*, Warr, P. (ed)., Penguin Education, Harmondsworth, Middx.

Kearsley, E. (1982), *Cost Benefits and Productivity in Training Systems*, Addison-Wesley, Reading, Mass.

Kempner, T. (1987), *The Penguin Management Handbook*. (4th Ed) Penguin Books, Suffolk, U.K.

Kenney, J. & Reid, M. (1986), *Training Intervention*, Institute of Personnel Management, London.

Knowles, M. S. (1975), *Self-Directed Learning: A Guide for Learners and Teachers*, Cambridge Books, New York.

Kolb, D. A., Rubin, I. M. and McIntyre, J. M. (1974), *Organisational Psychology - an experiental approach*, Englewood Cliffs, NJ prentice Hall.

Lawson,T. E. (1974), 'Gang learning theory applied to technical construction' in Stammer, R. & Patrick, J. (1975), *The Psychology of Training*, Methuen, London.

Locke, E. A. (1968), 'Towards a Theory of Task Motivation', *Organisation Behaviour and Task Motivation*, Vol. 3, pp. 157-89.

Luthan, F. (1981), *Organisational Behaviour*, McGraw-Hill Books Co., New York.

Lynton, R. P. and Pareek, U. (1978), *Training For Development*, Kumarian Press Inc, Connecticut USA.

Mace, M. (1958), 'The Supervisor's Responsibility Towards His Subordinate', in *Developing Executive Skills*, American Management Association, New York.

Maier, N. (1957), *Supervisory and Executive Development*, John Wiley & Sons, New York.

Mant, A. (1969), *The Experienced Manager: A Major Resource*, British Institute of Management, London.

Margerison, C. & McCann, R. (1985), *How to Lead a Winning Team*, MCB University Press.

Margerison, C. (1988), *Conversational Control Skill for Managers*, W. H. Allen, London.

Maslow, A. H. (1970), *Motivation and Personality*, (2nd ed), Harper Row, New York.

McClelland, D. C. (1961), *The Achieving Society*, Van Nostrand, Princeston, N. J., New York.

McGhee, W. (1958), 'Are We Using What We Know About Training', *Personnel Psychology*, Vol. II, PP. 1-12.

McGhee, W. & Thayer, P. W. (1961), *Training in Business and Industry*, John Wiley & Sons, New York.

McGregor, D. (1961), *The Human Side of Enterprise*, McGraw-Hill, New York.

Melford, A.T. (1962), 'On Changes in Performance With Age' *Lancet*. Pl.

Melrose-Woodman, J. (1978), 'Profile of the British Manager' *British Institute of Management,* London.

Miller, G. A., Galanter, E. & Pribram, K. H. (1960), *Plans and the Structure of Behaviour*, Holt, Rinehart and Winston, New York.

Miller, H. L. (1964), *Teaching and Learning in Adult Education*, Macmillan, New York.

Miller, R. B. (1967), 'Task Taxonomy; Science or Technology', *Ergonomics*, no. 10.

Mills, W. F. (1972), *Learning*, (2nd ed), University Press, Cambridge.

Miner, J. B. (1969), *Personnel Psychology*, Macmillan, New York.

Mintzberg, H. H. (1973), *The Nature of Management Work*, Harper & Row, New York.

Nadler, D.A., Hackman, J.R. & Lawler, E.E. (1979) *Managing Organisational Behaviour*, Little Brown & Co.

Neiss, V. (1977), *Cognition and Reality*, John Wiley & Sons, London.

Nobbs, J. (1983), *Sociology in Context,* Macmillan Education, London.

Nowaday, R. T. (1979), 'Equity Theory, Prediction of Behaviour in Organisations', in R. M. Steers, L. W. Porter, (ed.), *Motivation and Work Behaviour*, McGraw-Hill, New York.

O'Connell, B. C. (1973), *Aspects of Learning*, G. Allen & Unwin, London.

Osgood, C. E., Suci, G. J. & Tannenbaum, P. H. (1957), *Measurement of Meaning*, University of Illinois Press, USA.

Ottaway, R. N. (1980), *A Taxonomy of Change Agents* (3rd Ed), Department of Management Sources, University of Manchester Institute of Science and Technology. Manchester.

Pavlov, I. P. (1927), 'Conditioned Reflexes', Oxford University Press, London, England.

Pedler, M. (1983), *Action Learning in Practice*, Gower, Aldershot, England.

Pepper, A. D. (1984), *Managing the Training and Development Function*, Gower, Aldershot, England.

Peters, T. J. & Waterman, R. L. (1982), *In Search of Excellence*, Harper and Row, New York.

Pettigrew, A.M; Jones, E.R. & Reason, P.W. (1982),*Training and Development Roles in Their Organisational Setting*, Training Division, Manpower Services Commission, Sheffield.

Pfefer, J. W. & Jones, J.E. (1977), *Reference Guide for Hand Books and Annuals*. University Associates.

Reothlisberger, F.J. & Dickson, W. J. (1939), *Management and the Workers*, Harvard University Press, Cambridge, Mass.

Richardson, J. & Bennett, B. (1984), 'Applying learning techniques to on-the - job development', Part 2, *Journal of European Industrial Training*, Vol. 8, no. 3, MCB.

Robinson, K. (1985), *A Handbook of Training Management*, Keegan Page, London.

Rogers, C. R. (1951), *Client-Centred Therapy*, Constable, London.

Rogers, C. R. (1967), *On Becoming a Person*, Constable, London.

Rogers, C. (1969), *Freedom to Learn*, Charles E. Merrill, Columbus, Ohio.

Rogers, C. R. (1970), *Encounter Groups*, Constable, London.

Rosenzweig, K. (1974), *Organisation and Management* (2nd ed.), McGraw-Hill, U.S.A.

Schien, E.H. (1965), Organisation Socialisation and Problems of Management, in Katz, D & Kahn, R. (1974), *Social Psychology of Organisation*, (2nd ed), J. Wiley & Sons, London.

Segelman, L. (1973), An Organisational Analysis of New Reporting, in Mangham, L. (1979), *The Politics of Organisational Change*. Associated Business Press, London.

Seymour, W. D. (1966), *Industrial Skills*, Pitman, London.

Shannon, C. E. (1948), 'A mathematical theory of communication', *Bell System Technical Journal*, no. 27.

Shiver C. E. (1980), 'What Does Training got to Offer?' in Edmund, M. et al (ed), *Management of Human Resources*, Prentice Hall INC, New York.

Skinner, B. F. (1954), 'The Science of Learning and Art of Learning', *Harvard Educational Review*, Vol. 23, no. 1, March.

Skinner, B. F. (1965), *Science and Human Behaviour*, Macmillan, New York.

Smith, M., Beck, J., Cary, L. C., Cox, C., Ottaway, D. & Talbot, R. (1982), *Introducing Organisation Behaviour*, Macmillan Education, London.

Stammer, R. and Patrick, J. (1975), *The Psychology of Training*, Methuen, London.

Stewart, R. (1967), *Managers and Their Jobs*, Macmillan, London.

Stomberg, S.C. & Hill, H. S. *An In-House Training Program*, American Management Association, New York.

Tai, V. (1985), 'Update on Participative Training Methods', *Journal of European Industrial Training*, Vol. 9, no. 7, MCB University Press.

This, L. & Lippitt, C. (1966), 'Learning Theories and Training', *Training and Development Journal*, Vol 20, April.

Thomas, L. F. (1962), 'Perceptual Organisations of Industrial Inspectors', *Ergonomics*, Vol. 5, no. 1.

Thorndike, E. L. (1898), 'Animal intelligence; an experimental study of the associative processes in animals', *Psychological Review Monograph Supplement*, Vol. 2, no. 8.

Trost, A. (1985),' They May Love It But Will They use It', *Training and Development Journal*, Vol. 9, no. 7, January.

Turner, B.T. (1969), *Management Training for Engineers*, McGraw-Hill Book Co., New York.

Vroom, V. H. (1964), *Work and Motivation*, Wiley & Sons, New York.

Walker, J. W. (1979), *The Challenge of Human Resource Planning - Selected Reading*, (ed.), Human Resource Planning Society, New York.

Warr, P., Bird, M. & Rackham, N. (1971), *Evaluation of Management Training*, Gower Press Special Study, London.

Watson, J. B. (1924), *Behaviourism*, Lippincot, New York.

Watson, T. (1980), *Sociology in Context*, Macmillan Education, London.

Wiener, N (1948), *Cybernetics*, Wiley, New York.

Woodward, N. (1975), 'Cost Benefit Analysis of Supervisors Training' *Industrial Relations Journal*, Vol. 6, no. 2, pp. 41-45.

Wright, D. S. & Taylor, A. (1970), *Introducing Psychology - An Experimental Approach*. Penguin Education, Harmondsworth, London.

Zanger. J. (1985), 'Training for Organisation Excellence' *Journal of European Industrial Training*, Vol. 9, No. 7, MCB University Press.